Loving
the Light
Within

A Seeker's Guide to Channeling and
Your Own Spiritual Journey

Caroline Coulombe

(Translated by Jack Cain from the French:
Présence: La voie de la lumière.)

BALBOA.
PRESS
A DIVISION OF HAY HOUSE

Balboa Press books may be ordered through booksellers or by contacting:

Balboa Press
A Division of Hay House
1663 Liberty Drive
Bloomington, IN 47403
www.balboapress.com
1 (877) 407-4847

Because of the dynamic nature of the Internet, any web addresses or links contained in this book may have changed since publication and may no longer be valid. The views expressed in this work are solely those of the author and do not necessarily reflect the views of the publisher, and the publisher hereby disclaims any responsibility for them.

The author of this book does not dispense medical advice or prescribe the use of any technique as a form of treatment for physical, emotional, or medical problems without the advice of a physician, either directly or indirectly. The intent of the author is only to offer information of a general nature to help you in your quest for emotional and spiritual well-being. In the event you use any of the information in this book for yourself, which is your constitutional right, the author and the publisher assume no responsibility for your actions.

Any people depicted in stock imagery provided by Thinkstock are models, and such images are being used for illustrative purposes only. Certain stock imagery © Thinkstock.

Print information available on the last page.

ISBN: 978-1-5043-7036-3 (sc)
ISBN: 978-1-5043-7035-6 (hc)
ISBN: 978-1-5043-7037-0 (e)

Library of Congress Control Number: 2016920153

Balboa Press rev. date: 12/15/2016

CONTENTS

INTRODUCTION

In the present, presence shines.

I am touched by all those who search, be it in anguish or in joy. More than a book on channeling, more than a book on spiritual development, this work of mine is a book on life itself.

I strive to illuminate the perspective that trance work, in any form, requires work on oneself that is revealing and in constant evolution. Inner work, by harmonizing the personality, transcends the act of channeling. The reverse is also true. Channeling, in all its variants, informs and transforms the person practicing it as well as the person receiving messages.

The first part of this book is both intimate and theoretical. A number of personal passages have been woven into the theoretical elements. I have developed it as a mapping of the path I personally traveled to open myself to my mediumistic work even though it was not my first destination. Becoming a medium was a secondary path that I discovered without having sought it out. My original itinerary was simply a spiritual one and it still is—meaning that offering messages of light is only one of many avenues that I turn to in my quest for the divine. I am not attached to that one avenue. The development of intuition is just one more tool on the journey of return to the divine self. This return led me to write about channeling, or mediumship.

Throughout the book, you will find reflections, questions and exercises, humbly offered, to help with a work that is inner or sacred. In that respect, this book is for the benefit of everyone.

The second part is practical. Taking the theory of the chakras as a base, I explore several areas of life and provide a few daily practices designed to lead to spiritual awakening and prepare for trance work should you wish to devote yourself to that. Certainly, the result of all work on oneself, in looking more deeply within and being animated with a new energy, also leads to happiness, to an ease in living and to a more affirming presence, day after day. Even though my inspiration came from the chakra system, you do not need to master that system in order to profit from my advice.

Whether you are a light worker, a person consulting someone for channeling or just someone making her way along the path of the spirit, I am sharing with you ways of being and doing that can punctuate the spiritual journey like a scattering of precious stones and can prepare you for trance work if you so desire. Certain practices overlap, some lead on from one another and others mesh together. I present those that have been most helpful to me up to now. I don't know which ones are still to come.

What have been, are, or will be yours?

Take one from among those I am offering and taste it, take two and feel them both, take three, or take them all as your heart dictates. From experience, I know that all practices can be a working through leading towards redemption and a preparation for awakening as long as you don't become attached to them. In the West, the arrival is often taken for the journey, the end for the means, and the relationship with the supranatural is worshipped as if it were the ultimate relationship with God.

The divine is not a being to be seduced with our prayers, our dutiful work, and our sacrifices. It is not a being outside oneself that must be conquered. It is the essence of who we are.

The aim underlying a renewed study of the chakras, or particular spheres of life, is to continue to create in oneself a fertile soil for spiritual awakening as well as a burgeoning of happiness. Awakening and happiness are most likely to happen when life has been nourished in a satisfactory way and when the heart has been refueled—in that moment right after the moment when the inner struggle was still a distraction—in that moment when the greatest serenity has been cultivated.

Linear, sequential writing is not well suited to the full expression of my creativity. Instead, I entrust the expression of my message to my intuition, to the urgings of my heart and to the sometimes erratic movements of my personal history. In the end, all will be made clear through a multiple weaving together of various concepts and different levels of writing.

Writing is one vehicle among many for transformation. It leads me back to the pleasure of being a woman and of writing in a way that is sensitive and expansive rather than informative and rationally organized. It is important for me that what I have to say be charged with feminine magnetism.

I thank all those who were involved, either close up or from afar, in the completion of this writing project whether it be for their support, their caring, their teaching, or their talent.

My thanks to all those who believed in me and came to consult me or studied the art of channeling with me. My experience was greatly enriched by their opening and by their involvement.

Jean-Guy Nadeau, Jim Lewis, Gisèle Thibault, Tara Lewis, Marie-José Leclerc, Anne Leblanc and Suzanne Gagné reread the manuscript at different times in its evolution and generously offered thoughtful comments. Suzanne Gagné moreover reread the final version of the French book suggesting with great perspicacity the final invaluable corrections. A big thank you to one and all.

I am deeply grateful to Sergine Martinez and Mathieu Bélanger who stood by me during the rebuilding of the book's structure when I was feeling very lost and on the verge of abandoning the project.

A special thank you goes to Mathieu Bélanger for his superb layout skill and illustration talent that he brought to the digital book as a whole. Thank you Mathieu for your talent, your patience and your always-attentive ear. The digital versions of this book, in French and in English, are available on my site as both an iBook or PDF: www.carolinecoulombe.com

To Jack Cain, my translator, my sincere gratitude for his talent and his attention to detail in the rendering of my not-so-easy text from French to English. I feel that he has understood the essence of my work.

A sincere thank you to all the people at Balboa Press who graciously helped me complete this project and bring it into the world.

Finally, Jim, Tara and Solène, thank you for your unconditional support during the whole course of this project. And a special thank you to Jim for reviewing and editing this English version of my book. My thanks to all my family members and to my friends who continued to believe in the publication of this book even when its fate seemed uncertain.

At 52, I developed some cataracts, a rather simple and seemingly harmless health problem—at least in the eyes of those with good vision. At that moment, my life began to quarrel with me. It wasn't happy anymore with many things. It ordered me loud and clear to bring some order to how I saw life in general and to stop my endless grumbling.

In other words, it told me to stop resisting and it offered me the leisure of serving humanity. Nothing more, nothing less!

Part One

The Art of Trance
Learning it,
Perfecting it

To every thing there is a season and

A time to every purpose under heaven.

A time to be born and a time to die,

A time to plant and a time to pluck up that which is planted,

A time to kill and a time to heal,

A time to break down and a time to build up,

A time to weep and a time to laugh,

A time to mourn and a time to dance,

A time to cast away stones and a time to gather stones together,

A time to embrace and a time to refrain from embracing.

Ecclesiastes

The time has come for mankind to open
to all of life's dimensions...

Chapter 1

Writing

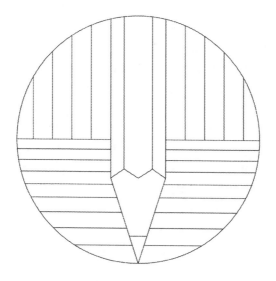

Communication is a way of going beyond our usual limits.
Anodea Judith

The Written Word

The power of words is immense.

I yearned for that power, achingly and for a long, long time.

Words for speaking about myself, words for sharing the power of my breath or its collapse, words for speaking of my suffering just as much as my happiness, those words had been stolen away in my childhood. They remained in the dark, hidden away, held back for a long part of my adulthood.

My estrangement from words, like my sadness, found its time of resolution. What I have to say does not reinvent me—it allows me to remember myself, to remember what I know, who I am.

I wanted to write so that my imprisoned words could escape, so I could read them and rediscover them, understand them and deepen them. I wanted to write for myself but also to offer a little of the light that I have acquired over time to those who might need it. It would take me ten years—ten years of solitary work that has stamped the words offered in this book with an intimate and transformative signature.

In coming to clarity and maturity, could there be a way of avoiding difficult paths? Could there be less suffering in freeing ourselves from the illusions that litter human life, so that the blindness that often darkens our younger years might be lifted? Certainly there can. Gently, without jolts, the ego must be allowed to die. But before letting it die, we have to know how to give this same ego all its room and all its force. However, this inner science seems to be totally lacking in our western world—a world that is materialistic and profane having been deliberately made profane.

For the moment, suffering remains the most effective way of growing and touching heaven with our fingertips. No container for the energy of the spirit will be found in a life that has been emptied of meaning. There was a time when certain religious rites obtained that energy by creating a welcoming structure for the sacred. Those rites are still intended to do that, but since they have been stripped of any significant connection with the intangible, they no longer comfort the soul. The light bearers have become rare and their pilgrim followers, people in search of their own divinity, have been abandoned, left alone in their quest for spiritual enlightenment.

In a materialistic world where appearances are more important than interiority, where doing and having trump being, the inner worlds are traveled on pilgrim knees with great difficulty. Isolated, the travelers are weighed down by the intensity of the pain. Their prayer, repeated through a crushing solitude, is wordless and disorganized, and often shifting to profane objects such as alcohol, money or even hyper-sexuality. But this prayer nevertheless rises up as a desperate cry for freedom just the same. This phenomenon is perhaps related to the birth of a new, liberal spirituality that is in direct contact with divinity. This spirituality is in response to a pressing need since the religious systems have failed in their mission of accompaniment. They were supposed to bring us closer to whatever is called God but they don't anymore. In this beginning of the Age of Aquarius, incarnated souls, mature and at one with the problems of humanity as a whole as well as with the problems of Mother Earth are supporting a more intuitive and broader view of life than ever before. And from that, perhaps, there may be as well the birth of a *new mediumship*—one that is more accessible, more within the reach of hands and heart, less an affectation and less stressful for those in service of the Light. The energy portals that support regular contact with Light Beings are ever more numerous.

Mediumship is a generic term that designates various ways of reading subtle reality or it may mean entering into contact with deceased individuals or with beings living in a vibratory field that is different from one's own. In energy readings, the modalities of perception change according to the person acting as the medium. Such a person is called a channel, a medical intuitive, a shaman, a clairvoyant, or a clairaudient, among other names. You can consult a glossary at the end of this book to become better acquainted with the various aspects of trance work and with the general field of divinatory arts.

Anyone who wishes can experience the awakening of his or her own mediumship which I will also call channeling, or, with a broader meaning, trance work. This work is developed through a focused attention to the body and its sensitivity. It also unfolds based on how the world of the inner mind is seen, observed, illuminated, and embraced. This inner seeing reveals the unity in all things. Did not Socrates tell us that knowing oneself was the same as knowing the whole universe?

Opening a channel of communication with a benevolent holiness is to find comfort formerly sought in church or temple and, in this opening, to discover words to speak of the experience. Such an opening is also a path to the awakening of consciousness.

Words Conveyed

From our life stories is born our experience.

In return, experience shapes our story.

This book—I have delighted in making it full of stories.

Some of them, luminous or dark, are about me. Others are those of individuals who came to me for channeling or who participated in my training seminars. They have agreed to speak about what they heard and to confirm the value of the messages that touched their lives, expanding and enriching them. Both the shorter and the longer tales, integrated with mine, tell of an experience capable of inspiring love and of adding substantially to the fabric that is the basis of our existence.

My book relates my awakening to mediumship—how it took shape as channeling and how it was launched into the world. Accepting to be an intermediary between the world above and the earth is to allow a flow of words from beyond oneself, arising from the heart like a prayer renewed, illuminated, never again lonely. Channeling proceeds from a very straightforward partnership with Guides. Mine are a representation of Christ energies. Angelic, Pleiadian, Arcturian and other energies can be contacted by various mediums or channelers. In this collaboration, images form and helpful messages are provided through the interpretation of these images. Sometimes, words that are also helpful come spontaneously as well as physical sensations and even emotions.

Through channeling, I do not attempt to help those who consult me to rise above their humanity but instead to rise above their small self to the true quality of a liberated human being. I want to help them to no longer be trying to change themselves but instead to return to themselves, to that island of their inner world where they can pursue and perfect the often unfinished task of constructing their ego, their *I*, that pillar of earthly existence. It is in this sense that I can say that I instruct based on the present without predicting the future. For those who come to consult me, I read a page of their lives so that they might be able to write the next page with more precision and serenity. From another point of view, I read it for them so that they might share that page with others offering love and mutual support. Almost all of them already have answers to the questions they ask of my Guides. My channeling simply helps them bring some order and clarification to their questions, sometimes confirming the authenticity of their decisions and their actions. I do not try to lay a possessive hand on the messages that pass through me. Each reading lightens and transforms me personally, bringing clarity to me as it does to the person consulting me. I am not attached to the message. I just let it pass through and meet the needs of the person it is addressed to. In this way, I become more available and more likely to help, sustain, and guide. This is what I have to do for the moment. I do this in collaboration with the Light. Who knows where this journey will take me?

> ... no individual, even the most generous, can cause another person to be spared the solitude of human destiny. One day or another, we all simply have to open our wings and accept that we are, as Sartre phrased it, condemned to freedom.
> Ginette Paris

More than thirty years of work as a psychotherapist and then as a clinical sex-therapist have allowed me to understand clearly the deep emotional life of the human being. All the beauty of the human lies just in that. It is certainly not a situation that requires fixing. Emotions distill creativity and support the growth of the soul. Once my heart was more open, I had a greater ability to deeply feel emotions of all kinds and intensities along with their infinite richness. I am not inclined to shy away from them as much. I don't spare praise for human feelings anymore. I oppose my associative mind more directly—that trickster who sidetracks me, who knows so well how to object to life, and who disguises his suggestions in words of love—suggestions that remain just illusions. My heart is still able to love even when it continues to be unable to attain unconditional love because its opening is too constrained, because its expression is cut short. May it soon be free...

Emotions experienced with humility and simplicity make possible a penetration into deep layers of the divine in oneself, as if a sacred fluid irrigated the quality that carries them.

Whether presenting in-person trainings or offering here in this book some directions for working towards opening one's own channel or cleansing a channel already opened, I aim to help those who wish to reclaim a birthright that many have forfeited—the right to live with an open heart and to establish more concrete and deeply comforting bonds with the Light. I went back to my own journey and identified its principal steps. I found myself called from beyond doorways, sometimes so narrow, they tore away at my heart. They were closed, imposing, and imprisoning. I learned, and I continue to learn, how to open them and to cross their thresholds. Behind each one there awaits a renewal—a breath of life. The sense of my existence is thereby clarified, woven together more solidly, as I move from trials to successes, from darkness to light, from awkward words to ones that are inspired. And from suffering to happiness. Until the point at which the wheel of this dualist life, relentlessly careening from one pole to the other, offers once again an agony, a challenge or an adversity. What one has garnered must be revisited constantly. However, it accumulates and solidifies with time. Hope gives way to more and more certainty; freedom replaces slavery.

In any work of awakening, in its patient and intimate working away, the essential is to never lose sight of the fact that the energy which moves up and offers a taste of ecstasy to the soul must necessarily move back down. Just as *the fall* must be followed by a movement back toward heaven. Balance returns. Renouncing delight leads back to our earthly home. Slowly, our home prepares for us, in the real world and in the body, the next contemplation. The mission of inner work is to accomplish the opening of the heart.

Chapter 2

Seeing

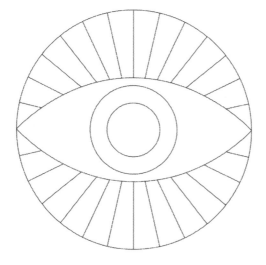

*A person who falls ill must dance with the illness through
what life offers so that the affliction, caught in the rhythm
of new, healthy vibrations, has every likelihood of being
returned to the norms of health.*
Annick de Souzenelle

Blindness

It was the beginning of September 2001 and the weather was magnificent. I was sipping coffee as I sat on the patio of a restaurant in Outremont.

Absentmindedly, I had just been cleaning my reading glasses. For some time, I would find myself repeating this procedure several times a day, to no avail. I was no longer seeing clearly. Finally, bringing all my attention to this mechanical movement, I realized that the cloud that I was trying to wipe away was still there in front of my left eye, even with my glasses off. I put my hand over my right eye and the shadow caused by the cataract in the other eye revealed itself for the first time.

On that beautiful autumn afternoon, so full of sunshine, the full extent of the discomfort which had crept into my days became clear and suddenly my life swung toward a new aspect of reality. A door was opening before me, inviting me to move through a certain something. Apprehensive and resistant, I tiptoed in. This illness is not all that serious. It does not imply some future fatal outcome or handicap; in fact, it is only a little incident along the way. I accept that. Cataracts are such small everyday things for seniors! However, they were showing me that something was no longer quite right in my body and therefore in my life. I needed to think about what it was. I could not simply assume it was due to aging. Early fifties is too young to be developing cataracts.

Waiting for an exact date for the operation and with the problems caused by a less and less competent vision, I began to worry and I felt really vulnerable. You have to look at it from the other side in order to be aware of the considerable damage caused by these little clouds. For the healthy, those with good vision, cataracts are invisible and therefore don't exist. With damaged eyes, the vision clouds and begins to hide what is essential and necessary. Cataracts are huge seen from the inside; quietly and steadily they gnaw away at the field of vision in front of you, figuratively and actually.

It wasn't long before I was negotiating a deal with this situation. I would find solutions other than surgery and triumph over the threatened darkness. I had to act quickly otherwise the clouds in my eyes would gain ground and I would have to undergo surgery too soon for my taste. I had gone back to school and it was demanding. I certainly had no time to be slowed down by altered vision or by undergoing an operation.

I hoped that with certain approaches of alternative medicine I would be able to slow down or even stop the process of my eyes' crystalline lenses becoming opaque. I wanted to find the energetic causes of the attack on my vision. I learned that this problem derives from a deficient assimilation of calcium or an aberration in this process which are conditions that can also cause arthritis. I was also able to understand better why I wasn't able to adapt to light—be it from the sun, at nighttime or artificial light. I gathered information, did research and my eyes continued to cover over and cloud up. I had not reached the underlying cause of this affliction.

Several times, in front of a mirror, I tried unsuccessfully to see what was not visible. Rebellion almost always accompanied this exercise: "Why me? Why that? Why has my body forsaken me?" My heart felt torn up, my eyes *teared up* and clouded over. They refused light that was made dazzling by the kaleidoscopic effect of the cataracts. And then, the operation having been put off for bureaucratic reasons, almost total darkness invaded my activities, my work, my studies, and my life. All I was able to do was to contemplate this strange health problem that was as disturbing as it was enigmatic.

Whether or not I was going to undergo an operation, I had to decipher the language of my eyes—their message. All distractions gone and vulnerable in my day-to-day life, I entered a deep existential suffering. Since this suffering had been with me for many long years, I had learned to set it aside. I no longer really lived in my inner world nor did I maintain a effective contact with the external world. The decision to complete my university degree gave me a new direction and brought a breath of fresh air to my work, but it wasn't enough.

When the body suffers, the eyelids close. When you are unable to carry on any longer, you fall to the ground and your eyes close. It's the same when the soul is suffering, it's inner eyelids close. For me, the cataracts acted like an inner eyelid, bringing darkness so that I could finally stop and recuperate, right in the middle of my headlong flight forward.

A New Vision, a New Life

This illness called out to me in a way that was crystal clear. It posed and imposed a basic question: "What is happening to your connection with the Light?"

I was undergoing a loss of adaptability to sunlight, street light, night light, lamp light in all locales. I was aware that I was no longer adapted (had I ever been—really?) to the shadow of my secret world, to my inner light, to the human, or to the divine.

I had lost my way in a *no-woman's land*. Outside, the colors of nature became less precise, less brilliant, long before the grey of the cataract interfered with the look that I laid on life. Even though I had retained a healthy ability to sometimes laugh, to amuse myself, to wish for a happy life, my joy had dimmed as the colors had dulled.

I felt isolated and isolated I was. I was paralyzed, imprisoned in a formless fog, in a grey, open-air prison right in the middle of my life. Locked away, I had taken a *dim view* of life. If I had been working full time, I would have had to confront on-the-job exhaustion—a burn-out. Working for myself and being in charge of my own schedule and professional obligations allowed me to make my way through this period of my life without medication, without too many unfortunate consequences. I was studying and working part time, but I was living full time; my heart was exhausted and my mind was out of breath. I was suffering humanly and spiritually. The movement of my spiritual search had slowed, almost stopped, from a growing sense of confusion, from a loss of contact and meaning. Cataracts were the pregnant symbol of this lack of direction and dynamism. At the same time, they acted as a drive that redirected me once again toward myself.

Human and spiritual polarities had slowly converged, coming together at a central point represented by my eyes. As we learn from Annick de Souzenelle in her *Le symbolisme du corps humain (Symbolism of the Human Body)*, the eye symbolizes the transcendent vision of the world, the vision of the world in its full divinity. Since physical, material life becomes aware directly of emotional suffering or of joy in being alive, and since material life provides signs of that awareness in a manifest and quantifiable way, I understood clearly as I traversed this hardship that the vision of my divine nature was deficient and that my ability to live joyfully was crumbling away. How was I to take on the full range of my human responsibilities when I no longer felt accompanied by the sacred, when I no longer recognized the divine spark within me?

It was not by chance that the part of my body that was calling me to order was the only one carrying in its name the vibration of Christ energy. The christ-alline lens lets light pass through, acts as a bridge between outside and inside worlds, while initiating and fostering the marriage of all parts of oneself. When this lens becomes covered, it shows explicitly that the soul is off track. Once uncovered, its egg-shaped form symbolizes a new birth, a new vision of a life that has again been made fertile.

Human substance—our body and our life of suffering and happiness—offers a choice of many roads to be traveled. But all those roads that lead somewhere other than into ourselves are sidetracks. The teachings of the mystics remind us that the most important discovery to make and to integrate is: "There is only one being—oneself." Having strayed away from my center for a long time while I searched for the perfect parent (disguised as a therapist) or for the perfect life-partner, and while I searched for objective, absolute truth, I had forgotten who I really was. I had forgotten who I was looking for and what I was looking for. I am a divine being and I no longer knew it.

I had to learn to stay very close to myself and to remain open. I had to be totally present to my inner life and to my authenticity. For a long time I had tried to do that but I had never mastered presence. And for that, no longer seeing the outer world was certainly helpful. Today still, that stage of my life, unavoidable as it was, continues to reveal intricacies of its richness even though certain secrets of its redemptory alchemy continue to escape my inquisition. I knew simply that I had to withstand helplessness and embrace my vulnerability. I know now, with great happiness, that in the gathering night, a light has begun to shine in my inner world. I know that it was all as it should be and that this hard road organized and fulfilled the sacred contract negotiated before my birth.

I was neither stronger than my body nor stronger than my fate. Both of these insisted on having me born from a new mold, a visual one this time, but just as organic and powerful as the first one. I would say that learning to welcome my vulnerability was the greatest gift of this second birth.

I underwent a first operation in the spring of 2002 on the left eye. A few months later it was the right eye's turn. My eyes, their darkened lenses cut away, were rehabilitated with two tiny pieces of plastic. I received a new vision for the rest of my days.

On the other side of that night, a morning of light awaited me—a renewed meaning for my life. In full awareness, I experienced the journey from illness to well-being and through that I was initiated into a better me, one transformed by a measure of being and of vitality. Losing a physical part of myself did not diminish me, it illuminated me. The blindness in which I awkwardly led my life began to clear away. A new vision sent me into the world a second time, more knowledgeable about myself and more creative, visionary even as to the next stage of my life. Not being adapted to the greyness of my life saved me!

Agreeing to the challenge that my eyes had offered me allowed its message to be established in my psyche, to be integrated and to transform me. Jean Claude Genel suggests that all traditions use the world of images as a tool for self-knowledge, and I would add for re-birthing. He says that representations of ourselves and of life provide for us through the art of visualizing— that is, seeing reality with a new eye—all the possibilities for a reconnection with the divine. Through my experience I had, in effect, developed a loving way of looking at the various dimensions of my reality, a way that integrated the spiritual aspect of my being.

I gained more self-esteem, and heart-felt qualities began to nourish my life, my relationships and my work. I learned to accept my presence, to let it emanate its distinctive color, and to no longer fear its breath whether it be discreet or penetrating. I learned to love myself with more care and integrity. I learned how to dance better among the challenges, dance with them in fact—challenges which life continues to set out before me, learning how to move more smoothly from laughter to tears, from sorrow to joy and to allow myself to sway gently back to sorrow again when that happens—without struggle.

In seeking healing for my eyes, I concentrated my energies on returning my soul to health, to stimulate an awakening to my true nature and a state of more confident opening to a divine that I recognized and loved. I believe that my cataracts could have been cleared through all the care received from various approaches of alternative medicine. But that didn't happen. However, deep down, the essential cause of my blindness was dislodged and I was able to be born again into a new vision of the world and of my world. As for channeling, it was not on the horizon. It appeared only as a probable secondary result— indefinite, distant. However, the memory of my spiritual identity, once reawakened, led me to my mission of service thanks to the inner work I had to accomplish in order to *see* again.

My eyes saw, my body opened, my vibration rose and my energy connected with its verticality.

Finally, my days were sunny again!

> I was born into great solitude. From the very moment of my arrival in this material world, I intensely felt a profound nostalgia for the universe of light that I had just left. This nostalgia faded only when my eyes, covered by a thicker and thicker veil, were invaded by a disconcerting darkness which created a silence and a transformative retreat into myself. Since then, my sight having been restored and my heart renewed, I am learning once again to let Light cradle my life.
> Passage from my diary

Chapter 3

Opening

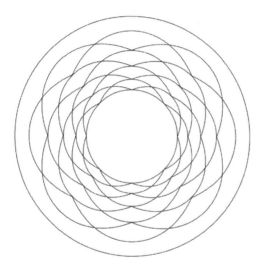

With the love of our mother Earth and the help of our father Sky, we are going to finally find a way to heal hearts and give back to the world its consciousness of the unity of all things.
Drunvalo Melchizedek

The First Time

Mediumship or channeling does not represent who I am. It's what I do, what I choose to do at this time in my life—among other things.

In all areas of my life and for as long as I remember, I have recognized my innate ability to perceive subtle energies, sometimes without believing in my ability and sometimes with a keen awareness of the benefits it can produce. Now I engage in it within a given structure that facilitates its expression. I owe it to myself to recognize this talent within myself and to name it because it is my reality. I believe however that the practice of trance work in its various forms does not necessarily arise out of talent but rather out of a clear choice.

I was born with a unique aptitude for contacting the Light. Very early on I remembered my life before this earthly sojourn and early on as well I yearned for that former life. In my twenties, under hypnosis, I saw a tiny little girl remember that place and feel a deep, aching sadness as she faced the exile of her heart. Over the years, I didn't know how the memory of that evanescent emotion that had accompanied my early childhood could be kept alive. Instead I thrust myself into illusion and into many artificial snares. Throughout a long quest on a winding road through the demanding seasons of my ordinary human life, I didn't always know how to maintain a perfect distance between opposites, between extremes, the highs and very low lows. Although always called, I continued along a large part of my path with the ultimate impression of a great solitude, convinced that my wandering would never end. Were I to do it again, I would stop sooner along the side of the road and I would try very hard to remember myself and my reason for being on

Earth. But there we are—I didn't know how to do that until I was into my fifties. And yet it is so simple! The road doesn't go very far. It stops right where we are. "Right under the sun" as is said in one of Serge Gainsbourg's songs from the 70s. Right where you are in the present moment; right where I was during all those years without memories. I made my life a quest when I had already arrived. Everything was being accomplished—subtly, slowly, perfectly. I had only to collect myself and extract myself from the outer world and its demanding performances. In the present, presence shines. Present to oneself, present to one's inner life, present to others and the world, present to the subtle, luminous energies around oneself.

One day the forgetting lifted, like a morning fog, clearing my inner eyes. One day, after many detours and much inner work, my consciousness awoke to what is. Blessed with a direct call, I began to see, and to remember myself—remembering perhaps even my life's mission. It was a Tuesday afternoon and I had stretched out for a short rest. In a state of deep relaxation, I was able to receive the visit of the Light. It filtered into me, smooth as velvet, truly exquisite, as if my body had been touched on the inside with a light but strong and penetrating vibration. About half an hour of intimate contact with this luminous Energy turned my life upside down forever. Enthralled, delighted by this Presence, my body revealed its strong power of concentration in the present moment and its entire strength of expansion in space. It is through the body and its sensory nature that the greatest spiritual openings come about.

Such encounters cannot be improvised but must result from long preparation—a preparation that is never complete. It proceeds one stage at a time and not necessarily following the planned order. The state of grace brought by such a visit fades and is sometimes very difficult to find again. It makes me think of the happiness of *falling in love* and of the loss of those first butterflies caused by day-to-day life. Renewing the enchantment, recreating the receptive state that is needed for such a pregnant contact with the Light is a work to be conducted each and every day. Some days are better than others; there are dull days too. Accepting closing and absence is just as important as the exaltation of an opening.

> *You don't know how the light feels or what it thinks... It is too immense for dreams, too persistent for loneliness. From dawn to dusk, it touches you with its million, tiny, fragile wings.*
> Lorna Crozier

A few days after this encounter, a medium whom I had consulted informed me that she had a message for me. Although I had spoken neither to her nor to anyone else about this experience, she tossed out the following to me: "He wants me to tell you that, the other day, it was Him." It was Joshua. He referred to Himself by this name in my first deep trance.

We had agreed, she and I, that she would help me reproduce, at will, a contact with this Energy that seemed to have been a chance occurrence. I must confess that I showed up at her place with a lot of expectations and a lot of naïveté. I stretched out on the sofa in her living room. She guided me through a very simple visualization and I was able to find once again the state in which a luminous presence had surprised me the week before. I was very relaxed, totally conscious and listening intently to my body which was becoming more and more numb and, at the same time, extremely alert. My heartbeat slowed down and a vibration began in my belly and then moved up. A pathway literally opened upward, extending past my head. I had the impression of being very tall. I became spacious, open, attentive—simply observing without emotion. Like the first time, thanks to the pathway created by relaxation and welcoming, I felt a Presence descend into me, penetrating me very gently. Little sparks scattered through me, in my head, then in my chest; they lodged in my physical heart. The taste of this light sparkling rain is delicious—a nectar of light. I became totally impregnated by materialized joy. I let myself be carried, transported. I encountered no resistance, no fear. I asked this manifestation: "Who are you? What is your name?" The response was immediate, spontaneous, "I am Joshua."

In the center of this space of love to which I had offered myself, Christ frequencies represented by the name of Joshua settled into me, and I was loved... infinitely.

> "Now, I know that you are praying to Me. I know that I have a place in your heart. And I, in my heart, have a privileged place for you, because even if you do nothing, this place is deserved. Even when you are not active this place is deserved. Life is free you see! I know that you are very active. And all those things that you do, you do them to Me through others. There is a great energy of devotion living in you and I am proud of it. Can you take the time to integrate this compliment that is addressed to you? So you can be fully nourished...
>
> You were wounded from having waited so long for love from your father and your mother, a love that seemed never to come. You believed that heaven and earth did not want you. But I, I say to you that if you are on earth it is because I want you in my service and because you have accepted. I am following your footsteps, footstep by footstep."
>
> Message from Guides

Beginnings

In the weeks that followed, I didn't quite know how to continue to open myself to Joshua's specific vibrations and also to those of my day-to-day Guides who wanted to make their presences known.

They had always been there; it was I who had not been available. I became available through my body—a body more awakened, more sensitive, more delicate in its inner quivering. I became available through learning how to look, learning how to see other than with my eyes. I managed to develop my inner seeing—broadening it, letting it expand through time and space. Trusting it.

My life had led me back to the moment of opening my subtle channel, a channel designed to receive luminous vibrations. Toward the end of my 40s, the movement of my quest for meaning had slowed down, almost stopped, because of an ever growing feeling of confusion and isolation. I had to withstand a lot of chaos before I could unfold myself, get up and get moving again, evolving in full awareness toward the straightening upward of my deepest being. Strangely, I didn't have the impression of having been broken. In my intimate world, even though many things had been damaged, the infrastructure had not been touched and my center was intact. However, at that moment I was unable to find the path to the central core...

If I didn't feel broken it was perhaps because my whole life long I had studied life—how to be, how to love, how to do— as well as I possibly could. I had been, in my own way, the best person that I could manage to be. I valiantly set about my labors, returning again and again this human soil from which

I had sprung. Straight from the primordial substance of my soul, I had crafted a universe that held together, that looked like it held together, a universe full of things both good and difficult, peopled by individuals I loved and who loved me. It seemed clear that a well-constructed life had prevented me from capsizing completely. The problem was that my life did not contain, within it, enough of I.

For a long time, I had mingled together the time of harvest and the time of love. I had wanted harvests at the time of sowing the land, desiring a sexual encounter and contact with God before opening my heart—living through many an autumn while forgetting to be reborn the following spring. I had wintered through many a long season, so asleep in a wasteland that I could no longer awaken at all, so asleep that my inner eyelids could open no more than a crack. I had certainly tried to repair things, to repair my past, to foresee the future—in order, I might say, to reassure myself. Sometimes, and perhaps more often than I would have thought, I had experienced fleeting awakenings in myself to pleasure, to happiness, and for the necessity of taking on the human substance of which I am made. But, in a cyclical way, I would always still slip back again toward a lack of complete presence to what is, allowing myself to be struck down by the *falling asleep* of my heart. This reflux movement was heightened at the moment when my eyes began to be covered, cataracts being a pregnant symbol of a lack of direction and dynamism. In truth, it may well have been that my eyes were covered because this movement was heightened.

Of course, from the outside things didn't seem so dramatic. My life seemed to be moving along happily. More and more however, I was stumbling over little things that slipped away, stretched out, took on so many doubts and unanswerable questions—little things as minimal as cataracts. They began to take up the whole space. The illnesses, the big and the little misfortunes and the non-successes seemed to be accidents along the way whereas they were the way itself. I am not speaking here of a suffering heaped on yesterday's aborted strategies, on all kinds of missing love, I am speaking of the tension of a heart that is not managing to open to itself, that forgets itself and forgets a sense of the divine at the same time. I am speaking about a life in full disarray while all seems to be going well when seen from the outside.

I am recounting these episodes of my life with a precise intention, one that is broader than just sharing my personal story, my whys and how's, my ups and downs and my inevitable rough patches. I recognize in all this the same type of crises that often bring people to the therapist's office. Each one of us feels very alone when we are right in the middle of the storm and its turbulence— just at that point where existential questionings include, in fact, generalized and necessary aches. It's important to recognize yourself as you move along. I think that if each one of us could comprehend with exactness the suffering of others and become involved without getting lost, healings would be more frequent and more complete—emotional as well as physical healings— because the loneliness would be less oppressive. As if, beginning from this place of loneliness where we station ourselves, the place where the essential work must be accomplished, we could finally recognize the tragic in human nature and be consoled by the sight of these islands in the world—separated but brought together by our inner eye. It seems to me that personal work would then be more likely and more convincing.

> *Freedom is the creative appropriation of limitation.*
> *Jeffrey Maitland*

Paradoxically, among all the illusions and all the disenchantments in which I was immersed throughout life's trials and throughout the not always conclusive repeated experiences of therapeutic, somatic or energy work, real lights have been lit. Sparse but precious little diamonds have been accumulated in my travel bag.

So, I had completed my classes and the emotionally difficult moments had facilitated getting through my exams! I learned to breathe, to meditate, to support my inner self, to let go, to get out of my head, to calm down my head. I didn't always manage it but I was evolving toward an acceptance of my life and its limits—limits that were slowly pushed back. I struggled less with my contradictions. Everything ended up being integrated, existing at the same time—fear and certainty, anger and compassion, retreat and opening, desire and peace, flight and presence.

My inner work and the guidance of my Guides fostered the rediscovery of a meaning to my life. And, following a few assisted trances, I felt able to offer energy readings to friends and then to individuals coming to consult me—thanks to the good reports which spread around about the help I was able to bring. Step by step, I understood how to induce an altered state that is receptive to Christ vibrations. These vibrations had called out to me, asking me to collaborate with Them in a mission of service and I had accepted. I learned how to structure the sessions, to create a protective environment for myself and for those who consulted me. And all of this through experience rather than through mastery of a technique.

The most important experience in the opening of my channel was the constant presence of my Guides and the inspiration received from Them. My sensitivity having been honed, I could, and I still can, perceive a sacred accompaniment in my day-to-day activities. Giving myself to that accompaniment is work for each moment, never assured, always to be pursued. Affirming loud and clear that this is a reality accessible to all is a challenge that I take up in the following chapters.

The divine plan! For a long time I have disliked this way of speaking. When I was little, it referred almost entirely to the sacrifice of our life, making us God's victims, stigmatizing in us the tortured image of the cross, and in fact separating us. Today, a part of the divine plan for me has been revealed to me, laying out my life experience in a certain direction and opening out onto joy and onto the sacred, onto the mystery of being more than this body, more than this personality, more than the numerous roles played out day by day, more than all the thoughts and all the words which are indispensable and at the same time beside the point. The divine plan, I now know, opens out onto the awareness of unity.

> *"All of this work in which We have accompanied you consists of greatly expanding your heart. You have integrated this work well. Now, your mission consists in redistributing to others all this love that you have received. You are capable of that because you have repeatedly been infused by light. One little step remains to be taken: You must affirm more strongly that you want, that you accept to give all your love. Say yes to your life, to your divinity and to service to humanity..."*
> Message from Guides

— Exercise and Reflection—

Stand with your hands held in front of you as if you were holding up a balloon that is neither too light nor too heavy.

After staying like that for a few minutes, the arms begin to tire. Allow a *no* to rise up. "No, I can't any more. I don't want to." It won't take long before you're going to have to let your arms fall. Shake them out and go back to the starting position. This time, say *yes* while trying to make the yes as authentic as possible. "Yes, I am holding the world in my hands. Yes, I am passionate about life. Yes, I say *yes*." You can hold out for a long time. It's almost easy and perhaps it really is easy. The yes, the acceptance is magic. Saying *yes*, is to say yes to the totality of life, to your body, to your humanity and... to your divinity. Don't skimp any more, don't believe in your fears any more—set out on the road in front of you. Whatever it may be.

We often hear the expression *mid-life crisis*. It definitely happens that an existential crisis shakes up our life in our forties, but more and more, this period of deep questioning of the meaning of life occurs at all ages—such as on the occasion of exhaustion on the job, a serious illness, the death of a loved one, a broken heart, to name only a few of the ways life uses to illuminate our spiritual progress. Energy opens us and wakes us up in all sorts of ways. These processes of renewal, frequent as they may be, are often misunderstood. Can you identify such a moment in your life? How did you treat it?

> *We sense a fault line, a crack in the impenetrability of certain mysteries. One day these mysteries will offer up their secret which will have been broken open through study, skill and relentless pursuit.*
> Jean-François Beauchemin

Chapter 4

Preparing

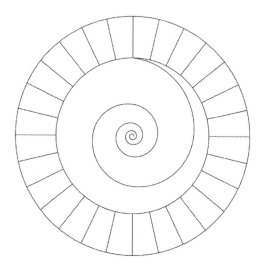

The privilege of a life is to be who we are.
Joseph Campbell

Is it not reassuring to realize, at the end of one's life, that it appears to be a work of art?
Albert Einstein

How It Was Before

I'm not entirely sure if what I experienced when my cataracts were developing corresponds to what is called the dark night of the soul.

It was clear, however, that the mood of my soul was moving downward. Why speak of the soul as if it were something other than me, as if I was divided into several parts, some human, some spiritual? Because the cameos, the portions of my life, some large, some small, which wandered in a semi-darkness of separateness represented my experience quite well—it was as though my being was fractured into pieces. Scattered images began to reflect more and more sharply what had been my lot since childhood: the impression of leading a double life, of being separated, being not centered but "off" in relation to my body and in my relations with others. The crisis that I was going through magnified this impression greatly. Sometimes, walking on the street, I felt so separated that I would see people strolling in front of me as if they were in a film. I saw myself as a spectator while life was passing by on a distant stage. I was stuck on the other side of the mirror.

I withdrew into myself. My link with the sensitive world, more or less effective in the past but very real, was in a shaky state. I had the impression of having wandered into a kind of purgatory or else having been shipwrecked on a desert island. I felt abandoned by heaven, and imagined that everyone was planning offensive strategies of rejection. But heaven never abandons; this rupture was my creation. Huddled into myself, I believed I was the victim of some injustice. I had lost all direction and all desire, not just sexual desire, desire for myself too, the desire that leads to action on all levels by constantly seeking a resolution—a resolution that could be ephemeral or deeply satisfying but one that would be always dynamic. Today I know that my condition was caused by a lack of direction. I know that I had come up against great suffering and that this suffering carried within it a *numinous* energy, one that opened the way toward the supra-natural.

Synchronicities and Presences

Although my mood was at its lowest ebb, I had accepted to return to school and my eyes, tools that were essential to my academic success, were deserting me.

I had decided not to be done in by my cataracts and, as I mentioned, I went looking for solutions of all sorts. Certain initiatives were perfectly logical such as consultations in acupuncture or homeopathy for example. Other components of solutions weren't necessarily about the health of my eyes but instead about my overall health—emotional and spiritual as well as physical. They were presented to me through synchronicities that I managed to decipher more easily than in the past. Sometimes, an angelic hand guided me, literally. This is how my going back to school had been decided.

From time to time books imposed themselves on me. They would wink at me; they would call out to me personally while I was browsing in bookstores: "Psst, you there. Yes, yes, you. Buy me." Sometimes I would feel like ignoring them but they called with such insistence that I ended up giving in to what they wanted. So, I bought them, giving myself over to a subtle guidance that abundantly bore fruit. It was a very special time—a moment of grace during which my Guides manifested in my life more substantially than usual. At the crossroads where I stood, They took me by the shoulders and had me change course, aligning me with a spiritual journey to which I had given my agreement. Now, I have the impression that, with their help, that is what I do for people who consult me.

I did some body work and took energy sessions using various modalities and I began to walk again. It was through my body then that my link to heaven began to be re-established in an obvious way. I took up meditation once again and began to feel myself at the center of my life. The affective dependency that I had suffered from for a long time had one final painful wrench before it finally unraveled.

> *I love my life because I adore the light of heaven which*
> *is ever present in me.*
> Tagore

It seems impossible that opening to the divine could be done without preparation, without a time of gestation and all the more because this opening cannot remain anchored in our human side without the serious work of integration. And so, the trodden path had led me to the exact spot where I needed to be and, honed by the problem with my eyes, a more practical work presented itself to open the next door—my mediumship. I was ready to welcome it in. In fact, that wasn't the goal I was pursuing at the beginning of this particular stage in my life. Instead it had to do with providing to the totality of my body, and the totality of its energy system, all the attention necessary for release in my eyes and in my intra-mind space. With the passage of time and the lack of responses to the questioning caused by the crisis that was battering my life, I plunged into sterile, obsessive and discordant internal dialogues. The moment had come to be done with all this negativity.

At that time, I took on a monumental inner work, something much more complex than before and one that was, at every minute of every day, a more targeted work of preparation for awakening. I was affected at all layers of my being, all at the same time. The various kinds of care I received, through their healing power, through their overall approach to the being and because of the tangible presence of my Guides, turned me upside down. More than that they tore apart my habitual way of being. Along with the surgeries on my eyes, they kept me in a constant state of tears and exaltation, laughter and vulnerability. I was not unhinged however, not disorganized, only capsized, turned around in all directions, turned head over heels. I was an uprooted oak thrown mercilessly into the storm. In the eye of the tempest, I experienced moments of peace, laughter, much laughter, renewed sexual desire, lightness and hope. It's entirely true. But very quickly, the moment of calm having moved on, I was carried away once again in the tornado's fury, further, deeper into the monstrous tangle of all the painful events of the past. All over again, but for one final time!

My body cried several times a day. I say that the tears came from my body because I had the distinct impression, each time, of being shaken by an independent organic movement. Do you remember the way Diane Keaton, in the film *Something's Gotta Give*, cries at the drop of a hat and without warning but with total freedom, expressing her broken heart with a brazenness rarely witnessed. And so! I was like her. I had no control over these brief but intense spontaneous sobbings, nor did I want to have any. I had held back my tears long enough. Also my body had come to the end of its silence. Its energy would never again be sacrificed. I would never again be sacrificed! Paradoxically, giving way to what was presented physically, even though often difficult and belonging to the past, created in me a greater skill in living in the present and experiencing its threads of happiness. I had never cried as much; I had never been so joyful!

At last, joy...

Sacred Accompaniment

I was not afraid, I didn't fear madness, and I didn't dread suffering either. Finally, suffering made sense.

Suffering revealed its secrets with disarming simplicity in spite of—or thanks to—its intensity. I tried, with difficulty, to adjust to losing control, to abandoning the head at the same time as my eyesight, then to recovering my eyesight but in a new way since the surgeries had made me short sighted. Everything bothered me—all at once. I was experiencing a state of great fragility all the time, flabbergasted actually. In all humility I can affirm that I demonstrated a lot of courage and valor. My life energy, always very strong, came to the rescue during this period of opening and energetic healing. I feel immense gratitude toward my Guides, their constant presence and wise guidance were some of the most precious gifts of my existence.

It is They who threw across the path where I was wandering, almost blind, a thunderous complexity, absolutely destabilizing, while at the same time ordering me to simplify everything. It is They who showered me with advice and practical suggestions. It is They who cradled me... Their help, their demands and their compassion finally rendered me capable of living my life with more balance and happiness, of awakening to my spirituality and to the marvel of my mediumistic talent.

Direct accompaniment by Light Beings helped my spiritual progress and made it gentler. I was not told to engage in disciplined meditation, or to adopt a strict vegetarian diet, or to withdraw from the world or even to take vows of celibacy or poverty. No, that wasn't suggested. I was told to love myself, to love my body and its feminine quality and to enjoy it, to appreciate what I had received, and to seek to live in abundance and generosity. It was repeated a hundred times that I needed to get out of my head and be present to my body, to bring joy to it as well as to my life—to mention only a few suggestions. I succeeded more or less, I continued to succeed more or less, but I always gave myself an A for effort. As for the advice to simplify everything, I just have to keep working away at it until I get it right...

Spiritual work leading to an awakening is like preparing a bedroom for lovemaking. You clean up, you decorate, you light candles and you choose the best music in the hopes of a sexual encounter. But it's not yet that. It's not a promise of pleasure. All is ready and several things can happen. Perhaps the sexual connection will happen and it will be satisfying or it won't. Perhaps it won't happen. The spiritual work we are speaking about here is not a promise of enlightenment. It's a way of preparing oneself for a state of being in love with life, with the divine, a way of refurbishing the inner world. And then, it's not awakening that comes but waiting for awakening... Awakening can only be prepared for, it cannot be worked over, induced, maneuvered. Grace is impromptu, instantaneous. It is not ordered, it is welcomed.

Spiritual awakening, which can be said to be a way of becoming fully present to what is, can very well be experienced without opening a mediumistic channel. But, the state of trance must be experienced in and through a spiritual journeying. *Knowing things* about spirituality is not being spiritually awakened. This distinction is often unrecognized by mediums and those who consult them. The need to accomplish a spiritual journeying that is illuminated and yoked to a work on emotional experience is the foundation of the divinatory arts. That is the essential message of this book.

> *"Great certainty in you at the moment. As if you knew in your heart where you were going. You are not in a hurry. You walk calmly because you know you are accompanied. At the same time, you are inhabited by duality which makes you ask a lot of questions. Ambiguity appears when you begin to reason. When you take the time to properly center yourself, you have no questions. Before, everything was complicated; now you have simplified your life and you don't want long explanations anymore. You have thrown things out, you have made room."*
> Message from Guides

Sacred Accompaniment—an Assessment

After several years of personal growth, of inner alchemy, my feeling in relation to this deep and exceptional work is one of healing.

A healing of the heart and a restoring of the damaged connection with my inner world and, consequently, with the outer world, have changed my life. I experienced a reconciliation with myself and with my own light, passing through the dark paths of almost all facets of my being and of my life in relationships and in society. It will have taken several years and it will take several more to integrate the work that has been done and the work to come. Integrate means managing to put back in place at the center of oneself the healing and the personal growth that accompanies it. One must take full ownership of them, with their limits, with their defects, but also with their own rhythm, their great rightness and all of their splendor!

I had to learn one little daily lesson at a time—learning what it meant to have an open heart and learning to keep it open in the face of adversity just as much as in the presence of love. It was not enough to have it opened by a luminous hand in a sacred space, which is already, I agree, really significant. These moments of great healing which are so spectacular, so extravagant and to which people cling so strongly—to which I clung to the point of almost forgetting my responsibility in this luminous process—are nothing in the end if we don't, in all humility, integrate them into our humanity. Assisted healings are nothing without the work of making them one's own. They are nothing more than a helpful nudge.

I had an intellectual and spiritual apprenticeship to engage in and I applied myself to it with devotion. I sincerely believe that I had been guided to certain specific places in order to experience in them an absolutely harmonious manner that combined suffering, opening the heart and education in the ways of life and spirituality. I can no longer affirm that my first choices, established perhaps before my birth on earth, are full of errors because they are as exhausting as they are beneficial.

The Spiral of Life, a Thought about Integration

Life is not simple and linear like time in the way we think of it. It is complex and its various facets are numerous. It is mysterious and secretive, glorious and imperiously stubborn, and as orderly as it is wild. It is stirred up with eddies and storms that unfurl over us in an apparently chaotic fashion. However, these movements never alter the fundamental organization of the life energy. Life, in fact, is deployed within time in the manner of a spiral. It seems to turn in a circle, fold back upon itself, turn backward, giving rise to emotional states felt to be anachronistic. Trials and tribulations follow on each others heels and share the same qualities, offer the same lessons, scratch away at the same wounds.

However, they never occupy quite the same inner space since a spiral is not a flattened out circle. Instead it is an open and dynamic curve that moves further and further from its starting point. It is a long Ariadne's thread curved back upon itself, enlivened by flow and counter flow. The ordeals and the closures as well as the joys and the advances always seem a little higher up, a little further away on life's helix. They get inscribed in our existence in a perfectly orderly fashion, each movement of expansion being preceded by a movement of contraction followed again in its turn by an expansion, and so on, to infinity. When I observe my life up close and when I identify a series of crises and moments of being down, I owe it to myself to take into account the happinesses, the numerous successes, and the flights of joy which have also punctuated it.

— Reflection—

Suffering Prepares Us Because It Obliges Us to Work Inwardly

Suffering slowly dismantles acquired defense mechanisms even if the illusion persists that these mechanisms are created by the suffering itself. Suffering reveals the separation and duality in which all life is at first experienced. It unmasks fears and resistances by exposing vulnerability. It cracks the tightly woven and therefore darkening fabric of the septum between the conscious and the unconscious, between the invisible worlds and materiality. A new perception of reality bubbles up in the mind and in the heart.

You might say that joy is just as transformative as suffering. But if I were to ask you to name several big moments of deep joy in your life, you wouldn't find it so easy to do. On the contrary, moments of sorrow and significant difficulties come to mind easily. They have more weight, last longer and are more demanding. They force you to take charge of all aspects of your emotional life, of the search for solutions and even of the quest for a richer meaning to your life.

Which were the moments when you experienced the greatest transformations? Do you know how to decipher signs of life, the meaning of synchronicities and of specific life events in your professional life, in your emotions and in your relationships? Do you feel accompanied by luminous Guides? Sacred accompaniment is sometimes impressive. But our invisible Guides have more than one trick up their sleeve in order to bring us back to ourselves. The signs that They present us with each day are often very simple—a book, a physical discomfort, a loss that may be weighty or trifling. Stay watchful!

Chapter 5

Understanding

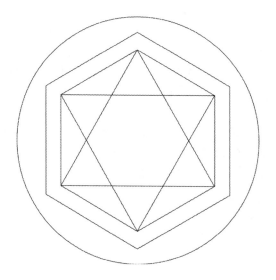

...while in their primordial condition humans possessed an instinctive knowledge of the sacred unity and profound interconnectedness of the world, a deep schism arose between humankind and the rest of reality with the ascendance of the rational mind. The nadir of this development is reflected in the current ecological disaster, moral disorientation, and spiritual emptiness.
Ervin Laszlo

The Scales Tip Back—from Masculine to Feminine

The advent of the rational mind, of science and of technology has brought much to humanity. It has been a necessary step in humanity's evolution.

This was a logical progression from a few thousand years of patriarchy, but, contrary to all logical expectations, it continues, with its limits and vicissitudes. It is a masculine way of addressing life and of choosing an action mode based on competition, perfectionism and consumerism. Does the pendulum need to return to a more feminine way of living? How to save the earth from eventual destruction? What would bring a better understanding of our lives, giving them meaning and a new spiritual direction?

The West deified the head and continues to idolize it. "I think, therefore I am" is how the seventeenth century philosopher, in his very Cartesian way, put it. Rationalism and the scientific mentality got imposed and technology complicated our daily life while making it a lot easier. I wonder what would have happened if the affirmation had been: "I have a body, therefore I am."

In the course of the last century, even though the victory was not total, women made enormous progress socially, professionally, and economically while femininity lost ground. In this world which has set itself up to be masculine first and foremost, and which struggles to remain that way, in this post-feminist era where the gains are not as numerous as it might seem, the subject of femininity remains borderline, almost taboo. Clearly, I am speaking here of the inner feminine reality, not the sometimes grotesque appearance of a body object, disguised as a sexually acceptable and allegedly desirable image, perfected by Photoshop or with a good deal of surgical assistance. The emotional debacle of a being whose body has been denied in order to conform to a stereotyped cultural expectation may seem masked behind appearances but sometimes it is all too clearly visible. No, I am not speaking of the outside, I am speaking of the inside.

My intended purpose is not social or economic, which in itself would not be insignificant. Writing extensively on the situation of women is still important, even urgent. For the moment however, my contribution concerns the quest for feminine power. The essence of this very much inner power is not to be found in the rational mind but in the body. This is true as much for men as for women. The body is the first destination of a spiritual journey, the first threshold to cross for the man or woman who seeks to approach the divine. Popular sayings are always very eloquent—when for example we speak of devoting ourselves *body and soul* to one of life's projects! The Orient bears witness to this necessity by offering yoga as a first step toward awakening, or, perhaps I ought to say, as an essential means for awakening.

My reflections have been greatly enriched when I read a very interesting book by Marion Woodman, *Addiction to Perfection*. In it she shows brilliantly how many centuries of patriarchal authority have caused lack of body awareness, excessive investment in the rational and intellectualism, and the establishment of material and competitive values. Femininity, because of its creativity and its values of the heart, because of its movement that is both expansive and more incarnate, was suppressed and thrown on the rubbish heap. Even after years of struggle, women are not flourishing more as women. They are scarcely much happier sexually. Among other things, the clientele at sexologists' offices bears witness to this. They have laid claim to masculine territory in an almost virile way to the detriment of their intimate life and their inner power.

Marion Woodman proposes "decapitating the wicked witch" who has set up shop in the head like some kind of Medusa—the goddess wearing thoughts like a hat made of a thousand snakes. So much so that her skull itself is a nest of vipers. She says: "When we intellectualize a problem, the body is cruelly neglected." Cruelly, this word is not too strong. The body is the carrier of the feminine in each one of us, both men and women; it is the feminine itself. Faced with abandonment, the body expresses its revolt in its own way. Through mental anorexia, bulimia or obesity, it can become a caricature of the man or woman inhabiting it. (Men are more and more affected by these illnesses.) The body can be afflicted with painful discomforts or mortal illnesses; it can suffer from an apathy in the senses. Often it just exists—without real sexual pleasure or great vitality. This is fairly symbolic of a civilization in which the feminine has been deadened, still denied, still abused!

At the moment when women devoted themselves to bring an end to the colonization of their bodies and therefore of their deep being and their sexuality, they first of all led a *head* struggle. They invested in the actual territory of the enemy and made it the first site of their holy war. As if they had traveled through Rome the rational—since all roads seemed to lead there—in order to arrive at their promised land. The initial movement toward freedom almost always takes avenues contrary to the intended effect. The child experiences great dependency before confronting autonomy. The adolescent throws himself into opposing parental and social rules in order to come to the discovery and affirmation of himself. Fusion often precedes differentiation in loving couples.

In the West then, women struggled like soldiers, they fought aggressively for their rights, and they demanded a social and professional status that was fair and reasonable as a first step toward their freedom. At the very beginning, this movement was charged with a somewhat masculine energy. Women won their place in the professional arena, but they worked like men— they were not working in a feminine way, and still aren't today. Installing a true liberty will coincide with a necessary return toward the inner goddess and her kingdom of flesh and blood without losing the externals that have been won. This has not yet been accomplished.

> *Macbeth and Lady Macbeth are metaphors of the masculine and feminine principles functioning in one person or in a culture, and the deteriorating relationship between them clearly demonstrates the dynamics of evil when the masculine principle loses its standpoint in its own reality, and the feminine principle of love succumbs to calculating intellectual ambition. Shakespeare's beheading of the hero-villain is, in the total context of the play, the healing of the country.*
> Marion Woodman

I suffered just as much as I benefitted from being 20 in 1970. My body had been largely neglected as I was being asked to concentrate on my intellectual and social development and put my body second in the war between the sexes. For a time, I had to go so far as to further abuse the sexual aspect of my already mistreated body to give myself the impression that I was enjoying a very relative freedom. In fact, the nascent sexual freedom tortured feminine psyches and many bodies engaged in self-discovery. Sexuality was experienced and is still experienced with the head, through its whims. The deliberate decision to make love, even when freed from old prohibitions, serves interests that are often different from those of the heart and even from those of the body. Sexual relationships and orgasms continue to be evaluated, tallied up, listed, regardless of their quality of being. The sensual is replaced by the virtual. Pornography, more accessible than ever, hyper-sexuality and pleasure on demand renew old contracts of slavery. What real progress have we accomplished since I was in my twenties? Unfortunately, the response to this question is not very encouraging.

The main losers in all these rebellions are the men. In the repression of the feminine in general, men too have lost contact with their feminine and they continue to seek it with variable success. Sensitivity and the body have been sacrificed to the rule of a patriarchal power that is particularly harsh toward its own protagonists. Men, like women, suffer deeply in their inner and feminine world.

Years have gone by and the hearts of many of us have stayed closed, having been alarmed by the battle for rights and the virulent demands of all the combatants. The body continues to silence its suffering while emotional insurrections, disguised as dependencies of all kinds, are all too frequent. Rationality is the most merciless judge there could be and effectively destroys the connection to the inner world—the world where life's meaning might be discovered.

For some, this provocative little detour in a book on spirituality might be surprising; for others, it might be quite out of place. However, it really takes into account the body-mind dichotomy that I suffered through in depth and which is very widespread. It is why, at the very beginning of a more direct working with the Light, the pruning of my energy tree was so important. Rationality must never be lost but it does need to be put in its place and kept within rightful limits. The head is a place to explore and honor but making it your permanent home is destructive. It was destructive for me.

A New Paradigm: the Integration of Masculine and Feminine

There is a great temptation to throw out the baby with the bath water. In fact, the masculine with all its good sides is not to be tossed on the rubbish heap as was done with the feminine.

How to find the right balance? In acupuncture, when an energetic element is *made yang*, it is said that there is a yin void. Healing takes place then by bringing energy to the yin so that the overabundance of yang can depart allowing the energy to flow more freely between yin and yang, between feminine and masculine. The pendulum will never be motionless; there will always be fluctuation. There will always be a movement back and forth between opposites. The movement of the balance arm can be calmed and can de-calcify. Trance work, based on the collaboration between the more feminine right hemisphere of the brain and the more masculine left hemisphere is a good example of an integrated model.

A more heart-felt and more healing trance work, one that is less focused on information and predictions, requires opening to a new paradigm. In their expansive and intuitive nature, mediumship, channeling and their various forms of expression are intrinsically feminine. In practice though, they are often conducted in a masculine way— by searching for precise, showy, effective responses using a rather cerebral technique and a framework that takes precedence over a felt sense.

Within a patriarchal paradigm, the divinatory arts, patterning themselves on religion, intend to rise up *into* heaven and leave behind the earth that is within. In such a paradigm, the process develops in an intentional manner. It is more static, it seeks to incorporate fluidity but its direction is already fixed. The process is set up, defined, structured and oriented toward a final result. This means staying with the process, and being in a given place, generally outside one's body. Learning a technique then is to allow oneself to be taken by an intended process that is known ahead of time.

In a more feminine paradigm, learning trance work is to experience a transcendent state fully enough so that it is really known from the inside and so that being in it, you recognize—paradoxically—its *unknowability*. In this state, you become very calm within the center of the self. Heaven is called and silence gathers in a space filled with the desire that heaven descends into your own inner earth. The attention given to rationality is brought to a stop gently and without rigidity. The heart is in movement and becomes *caring*. It opens and penetrates into the expanding inner space that is submerged in sensations. In these sensations there bathe: other people, the client, the past, present, or future, the visible and the invisible. The heart, not the intellect, is in a receptive mode permitting this process to unfold. Where will it come to? Nothing is foreseen in advance. The instrument (the channel, the medium) does not know where it is going. The body is involved, the heart opens, and there is a looking upward without leaving behind bodily support. Whatever happens happens. And that could be nothing at all! The masculine aspect integrated into this feminine state is found in the structure of the message given to the individual who is consulting.

Yes, Leave the Head Behind but to Go Where?

Being a Westerner and North American, I definitely learned to live in a rational way.

As long as I stayed that way, perched in my head, surveying the Western world through my eyes, a world so attached to the visual, to appearances, to representation—avoiding a more body-oriented felt sense, the quality of my life was very much whittled down.

As long as I was thinking in a deliberate fashion, trumpeting on high from my *hefty* interior my personal mix-ups and jokes, my body was left to its own devices. However, emptiness, the silence of emptiness, constitutes the only possibility of a conscious welcoming of the divine which is already within oneself. It lies there dormant, ignored. The seat of this emptiness is the body.

Calming mental agitation was only a concept at the beginning of my spiritual awakening. A concept that I actually was well acquainted with but which I had never really committed myself to.

It wasn't so much that I was afraid of the silence itself. Instead I was afraid of the purifying quality of the silence which was capable of having me contact more intensively certain anguish still resident in my body. Moreover, I was very attached to those stories in my head—the small or large dramas of my ego, my silent but verbal dialogues with people who I said I loved and who, inside myself, I sent packing. Besides, I was my worst victim. I gave myself little respite. I had no desire for all that to suddenly disappear. All the struggles that I wanted still to win, all the ego battles that needed to be waged, how could I accept to give all that up forever? A cutting away that I considered to be untimely and one that would have left me dumbstruck and terrified as I confronted the essentials of my life experience, terrified by the joy of life even more than by the pain of life. Eventually however I understood that if the inner scenarios dulled the real pains, they also distracted me from real joy. Do you recognize yourself in this portrait?

> *"First of all, you need to bring all this agitation in the head to a stop and calm the mind. Free yourself from your mental babbling and from your automatisms.*
> *Within yourself you carry a gnome, and also you nourish him with all kinds of unfortunate thoughts. He's a talkative little gnome—clever and malicious who tells you so many stories you are hypnotized and you believe those stories as you sleep standing up.*
> *Silence the troublemaker mind and let the silence pervade you."*
> Message from Guides

It would have taken me so much time to manage to reduce the mental chatter, and consequently to find a taste for joy—wanting it entirely within my body. And it's still not mastered!

Leaving the head behind, yes. But then where to go? To what forgotten or even unknown country? This land of flesh is first and foremost an emotional place. Emotions (energies-in-movement) live there along with their setbacks, their tears, their cries and their exaltations, all of it, everything at the same time. Pleasure, joy, anger and sorrow are the body's inheritance. This is why silence and healing can happen there. A real healing of the heart can be established in the body and by means of the body if you manage to listen to its complaint, as well as its song, with all the necessary watchfulness. You need to let the emotional life play out without impediment and peacefully. At the same time, the healing cannot really happen without a victory over the tumult in the head.

I knew that meditation, through which there can be a letting go in the head, leads to peace, but I had not understood that it reveals the body's territory. A friend who had meditated a lot even used the word *sweet* to describe the breathing that develops during deep meditation when the thinking has silenced its shrill and bewitching voice, a voice full of sour negativity and capable of creating emotional tidal waves. Our great challenge in being human is to taste the sweet joy distilled by the body, a body inhabited when cloaked in its highest quality—the quality of love. This challenge undoubtedly takes us closer to our divine reality.

Since I was having difficulty meditating, that is, really emptying my head, abandoning myself to the silence of my body and to my subtle life energy, I decided to at least moderate the wanderings of my intellect and to continue to think but peacefully. I *thought* therefore in my body. I literally descended into it. I would install my consciousness in my feet for example, or in any other part of my body and I would let myself float there. Calmly, my thoughts dissolved, letting me feel my feet, then my legs and finally the whole of my body both inside and outside. In this way, little by little, I conducted an owner's tour and what resulted was a better relationship with my physical reality—seen now to be dense and feminine. I made gains in vitality and in groundedness. I developed a greater body awareness and refined my contact with my sense of being embodied and the sensuality of that. The craft of focusing on something other than my deafening thoughts turned out to be of great help in facilitating my first trances.

I learned how to return to this state at will, in my stomach, in my heart, in my tired, aching muscles that I was finally able to relax, in my new eyes, in any spot in this body—a body in serious need of being loved. The more joy inhabited my body, the more it relaxed and the more the vibrations of my energy became modulated. My vibratory rate managed to increase in the same measure that for a long time it had decreased. I was no longer stuck in a specific way of being—a movement that was more ordered and less broken up had made its appearance in my inner world. High tides, low tides, shake ups continued to constantly transform the landscapes of my soul. However, it was transported more often by solar flares whereas so many dark hurricanes had ravaged it, and probably would ravage it yet again. Happily, the hurricanes became infrequent. More often the sun is now shining on my days.

My body was learning to become totally peaceful. Sometimes it would become paralyzed, in a *hypnogogic* state, a state supportive of contact with the Light. Duality being still an active element in life, deep and dynamic penetration of the peaceful inner seas, or even those that were stormy, seems only to happen in the joyful immobility of the physical envelope. The hypnogogic state could be defined by attention placed on the density rather than on the subtle energy since the intention is not to leave the body but instead to enter into it completely, to bury into it, and to open to an immaterial *elsewhere* beginning from the body's heart. As if we had been attached during the whole time of our life on earth to this material world and that there was no point in trying to leave it behind.

Understanding: a Quantum View

The Reality Is Complex, Infinitely Vast and Inhabited by Space

The universe, multidimensional and interdimensional, is an immense pool of energy, differentiated but unique. All dimensions of energy (light, absence of light, parallel worlds, past, present and future, to name a few) exist simultaneously within the same space-time continuum.

It is not distance or time that separates us from others or from our environment but rather our own energy frequency. In order to manage to *read* energy of greater or lesser density, greater or lesser subtleness, you need to change your energy frequency to bring it into resonance with a larger range of realities. The higher vibratory dimensions are less dense and the energy frequency is therefore higher. To reach it, your brain wave frequencies have to decrease—from gamma to beta, then from alpha to theta and even down to delta. The best tools for learning to contact higher vibrations are work on oneself and the calming of thought.

All energy can be perceived from its pulsation. All energy contains information. All energy is light. Even darkness is a variant of light.

A vast luminous energy, that is of the same nature as the light of day, close to electric light, undulates through all things all the time. Like a background fabric. A quantum link is created, the whole of life is reunited. Coiled in the heart where this energy takes refuge, knowledge of things unfolds easily because everything is connected to everything. Separation is an illusion.

An electromagnetic field produced by the biological processes of the body emanates from each person, thing and living being. Quantum physics has proven the truthfulness of this statement. The human body produces electricity because it produces energy. The various manifestations of the electromagnetic field correspond to the auras which are radiations from our bodies of different frequencies: physical, emotional, mental, causal and divine. The auras then indicate various components of the personality and of the being. They form an information center organized into a system that is highly sensitive and therefore perceptible, especially by the heart. This emission/reception system allows us to be in communication and to enter into resonance with everything around us. It allows us to communicate—that is to emit and to receive energy, to resonate with all that is, the way musical instruments do when they share the same space.

Janine Fontaine, in her book *Nos trois corps et les trois mondes (Our Three Bodies and the Three Worlds)*, explains that "the discoveries of modern physics are infiltrating the scientific world. Modern physicists, having become the new philosophers, are rediscovering an ancient view of the world, one that was established by mystics. From the beginning of this century [the 20th century], physicists have demonstrated that the particle, the constituent element of matter, can behave also like a wave. Matter contains waves and vice versa.

"Until now we have mistakenly considered matter independently from waves because, when we measure matter, the wave cannot be measured and vice versa. To such an extent that all that has been studied is our *Matter-Body* or *Particle-Body*. Our *Wave-Body* has not been taken into account. It is only known by sensitives who possess higher qualities of perception that exceed not only the perception of common mortals but also that of instruments."

Silencing the thoughts and calming the body create an altered state of consciousness allowing us to enter into either a state of meditation or into a state of trance of variable depth. When we are no longer in thought, our consciousness descends into the body and expands. It then joins the totality of what is alive and manifested, regardless of its frequency.

We have all had experiences of clairvoyance that go beyond simple intuition. Such experiences are not the exclusive domain of a few mediums or healers more gifted than the average person. Daily life abounds with extrasensory perceptions and *things-that-I-know-without-knowing*.

Almost all of us have answered the phone knowing exactly who was at the other end of the line. Sometimes it's logic that dictates this knowing, and sometimes logic indicates exactly the opposite. But we know. We know that we shouldn't venture into this elevator with this stranger. How many times have we shouted at ourselves, "Ah! I knew it but I didn't listen to myself." The habit of discounting what we know if we know it with our gut is acquired very early in life. However, our whole life long we perceive in an instantaneous fashion parts of reality that escape our understanding. As if they appear in a different location within our personality— a no-man's-land, a deserted far corner. This diffuse knowing is a rudimentary version of altered states of consciousness. Since it exists in each one of us, it can evolve all the way up to mastery of the art of channeling.

Trance work represents an intimate, dynamic and complementary relationship between the body, matter, life on earth and a vibration that is higher, more luminous, more vague or more precise depending on the skill of the channeler— but always a vibration that is very real. It is a dance that requires an always-fluid movement between letting go and doing, opening and serving, abandoning oneself and collecting oneself, touching the light and the human at the same time. It is a prayer of love that requires an unconditional and authentic presence in the service of the most elevated part of the being and of life. It is a moment of letting go in which masculine and feminine, divine and human are harmonized in the way two musical instruments are tuned so the vibration of one echoes the vibration of the other.

– Advice—

Consulting a Channeler or Doing Your Own Channeling?

Assure yourself that the person channeling, the medium, or the clairvoyant, does not harangue you and that she is grounded in reality and in her body. Trust your intuition: Is this person working for herself in order to increase her own personal power? Does she put your interests first? Do you feel comfortable in her presence? Ask yourself if what she says resonates as a higher vibration, a vibration of love. Does this person seek to dominate you?

You offer, or you are learning to offer, messages in the capacity of a medium, channeler or clairvoyant. Be sure to be grounded in your body and in reality. Continue your own inner work without interruption. Engage once again in your own therapy sessions at certain difficult moments of your life—at the time of a divorce or an illness, for example. Just because you are enlightened by the presence of your Guides does not mean that you don't need to be helped psychologically. I would go so far as to say that it is a duty.

Do your transmissions have a feminine character? Have you acquired a good balance between feminine and masculine in your personal life?

Chapter 6

Tuning

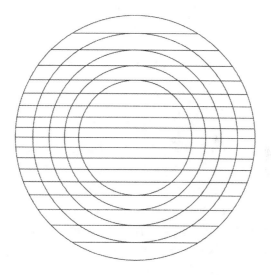

*...this wisdom that we must now develop in opulent societies
where psychological destitution is in dazzling ascendency.*
Ginette Paris

*The inner journey is an art, a cosmic game, a celebration of the
life that inhabits us; it is an experience of pure presence, deep
regeneration and intimacy with oneself.*
HO, School of Rites of Passage

Tuning Yourself, or How to Work Your Instrument

By assimilating into the totality of our personality the parts that are isolated or are imprints of psychological destitution instead of rejecting those parts, we create unity in ourselves.

The more the body is integrated, the more the personality is as well; the more the personality is integrated the more the body is as well. And the more the soul and the Self can make their voices heard and lead the way to an experience of the divine. It is often said that a singer, a musician, or an actor, has to work the instrument with which he sings, plays his music or his role. His instrument is himself and that includes, in part, his body. For the channeler and for all those who work therapeutically, the personality must be integrated, less polarized, and the body must be well harmonized.

In achieving harmony or attunement, various integration paths are available: Psychotherapy, body work and meditation, yoga, breathing exercises, walking, being present in daily life, as well as deciphering the synchronicities, hardships and joys of life itself. The divinatory arts, mediumship and channeling among others, are also ways of developing humanly and spiritually—if that is our intention.

Psychotherapy and body work, meditation and channeling, even though they are based on sometimes divergent techniques, have several points in common, the most important being the return to oneself. This return is facilitated by accepting the present as it peoples our daily life and by constantly cultivating a state of being present to oneself.

All the various ways of working on oneself enrich each other and complement each other. They simply move along side by side or they follow each other. They interpenetrate each other or overlap each other. They do not oppose each other. Each one multiplies the benefits of the others and fertilizes in its own way the inner earth where seedlings have been planted and cultivated. This is why a person can meditate every day, have a therapy session every week, receive physical or energy sessions often and consult a channeler occasionally—without becoming scattered.

Once the need for support has been recognized, the choice of meditating, consulting a channeler or therapist should be done by intuition, following the rhythms and signs of life.

> "... a channeler who plugs into a vibratory field of information accesses information fields that correspond to his highest vibratory level. His own nature as well as his idiosyncrasies (that is, his mental, emotional and spiritual distortions) invariably affect the quality of the information received.
>
> "Using a metaphor from the world of technology: A high quality antenna is indispensable to the decent reception of vibratory information. If the antenna is encumbered or deformed, the reception will be affected.
>
> "It is up to the individual reading the channeled information to determine its quality and precision."
>
> Words collected by Martine Vallée, Le grand potential humain (The Great Human Potential).

Psychotherapy and Body Work: Vivifying Human Light

Intimate Words

In the beginning, suffering separated me from life instead of attaching me to it firmly. For hours on end, I was adrift in therapists' offices relating my *being-ills*, seeking and finding words to bring to light these ills in their full seriousness. I put so much effort into inventing a way of talking about them that was more accurate, more explicit, and I did this even if it relegated the intrinsic causes of my problems and their designated creators to a host of more or less rational arguments.

Psychotherapeutic analysis, a feminine art, consists of separating the wheat from the chaff and of delving sparingly into woes with their attendant ins and outs in order to extract a manifestation of freedom expression. It is necessary. This work of clearing is fertile and fundamental. It supports conquering inner space thanks to a series of victorious deaths and rebirths, named and renamed with an increased awareness.

However, we must recognize that this work is essentially preparatory and organizational leading to the final work of healing. The day will come when the body has to seek its own words and find them. In the silence of working with the body or opening to the body, which is work that seeks to wash away the flotsam and jetsam of the past, in this silence of the awakening body, the experience becomes eloquent and reveals the best kept secrets—those which would yet have gone astray in verbal expression.

The Body's Words

The body is always right. It knows better than you do who you are and where you're at. It knows more about you than the professionals you consult, more than the doctors. When a therapist works with you, he ought to listen to your body's words (hear the hurts behind them) and not his own know-how in blindly following a technique that doesn't necessarily fit the mood you're in at that moment.

Sometimes the body decides that the heart is drowning in too many wounds, even if not all of them are all that serious. Thinking then comes to the rescue. This is not a movement to be rejected but just don't get stuck in it. The diagnosis that the body throws out into the center of a person's life responds to its own, often unfathomable, criteria. Looking for the meaning of what is perceived as a verdict, your head takes up the charge, lingers at the portico of your mind and projects a part, if not all, of its attention—always with great drama—on problems that are sometimes minor, sometimes important but not fundamental. Often in therapy, I have heard, or elaborated myself, long repetitive discourses which found their resolution in words that were very simple but infinitely more painful than the complaint that gets identified and gone over a thousand times. *Saying-anything-but-what-there-is-to-say* is a slow and fundamental process that serves to strengthen the ego in order to allow it, when the time comes, to courageously confront what is tragic in one's existence. This is an operation that must be respected, never skipped over, avoided or rejected.

Therapy using words is a patient and supportive walking through the mazes of an extravagant and complex delirium that masks, for as long as it needs to, the primary and sometimes unique pain. The mental agitation, distractions, accusations, dramatizations and scoffing of the sub-personalities act like so many security valves. At the pace that suits him, each person in therapy enters into a spiral of reflections and memories that lead him to the center of himself. However, in this founding kernel of the personality, the final expression of suffering must find its place in the body in order to become transcendent, in order to accede to the wisdom of being in its first instance— ontological wisdom.

Personally, I had never completely succeeded in letting go of my head and its numerous defense mechanisms before experiencing real healings accomplished by revelations emanating from my body. Before that, apprehending these revelations had been too painful. For a long time I wore my body like a confining and worn out garment, neglecting to listen to its words and its mysteries. I had never managed to completely inhabit that place marked with a maternal seal, my female ancestors having had to evacuate the abode of the body in the face of repeated rapes and violence. I too was in flight, fleeing in the direction of my head from the rape of my mind and its physical counterpart. Marion Woodman, once again from her book *Addiction to Perfection*, led me to understand that "when the maternal matrix is damaged, the child cannot root itself in its own body, and no matter how hard it tries to find security through the mind, it is always, on some level, dependent on others and therefore in fear of abandonment."

And Alice Miller adds in her *Ta vie sauvée enfin (Your Life Finally Rescued)*, that suffering in depression "... is due to being cut off from one's own Self, which was abandoned early on without ever having been grieved and which never had the right to live. Everything takes place as if, through the depression, the body was protesting the disconnection from true feelings..." It is not true feelings that are heavy for the soul, it is not expressing them in an engaged manner, with consciousness and a felt sense of the body, with connection. What also needs to take place is that words designating the truth be gathered together in the heart so that the gateway to the body can open.

Did I go all the way to the end of my deliriums and my mental fixations? Perhaps not... I accomplished this extensive work in a cyclical fashion, sometimes with a flare, sometimes with poignancy, but always with determination. At the end of each cycle, I was convinced that I had finished with the decadence of my inner theater. Then, new strata of life were updated, presenting their own resistances, their own hungers, their own heartbreaks in the face of the loss of even deeper parts of my ego. Numerous are the mournings to be conducted serenely as we grow old! One day, my body had me understand its essential complaint, a hunger for all things associated with multiple desires and nostalgias against a backdrop of humanity and finally I understood it. This never-to-be satisfied hunger, as I understood shortly afterwards, was hiding the call to divine reality which alone was able to quench my thirst and satisfy my appetite!

Words and Thoughts—in the Right Measure

Moving further into the body is not a rejection of rationality. It's a choice related to letting go. *A place for every thing and every thing in its place.* A place and a time for the head, a place and a time for the heart, a place and a time for the body. And a time for the marriage of these various elements in a reconquered inner space. Words and reflections have their legitimacy; they are necessary. They must be part of our daily life but in the right measure. And they must accomplish a work rarely undertaken: They must provide for the growth of our souls.

The realities of life present themselves to us with an infinite wisdom and they must be expressed by using words with great precision so that their meaning and the sacred within that meaning can appear. For a long time I have loved using Marie Cardinal's expression "words to tell it with." I love playing with words to talk about myself, words to tell the difficulties and pleasure of being alive, words for telling and describing and denouncing and revealing what is and what I am. I missed them achingly for so long! I love words that divide up the darkness and the light, that divulge the secrets of the night and delight the unfolding of the days. I no longer love words that accuse and lay their obsessed and obsessive thought on life, sapping its fluidity. I carry within myself reflections and words that delineate and situate my discontent and that of others, my happiness and that of others, and all this within the prodigiousness of life itself.

For the person who seeks a consultation, psychotherapy and body work represent spirals of reflection, or movements in the body. They also represent memories that lead him back to the center of his suffering from which there emerge words to speak about it. Thanks to a new, deepened consciousness, the light and the vibrancy of what it means to be human is vivified, and augmented. The acceptance of *what is* becomes possible. This essential stage in the work on oneself can lead to spiritual awakening.

The therapist, in her role, observes a certain distance that is loving and crafted. This distance implies a non-anxious presence when confronting stress, resistance or anxiety in the client. This is not indifference, or detachment, in the sense of not being implicated or *folded in* (an expression dear to Jules Bureau, author of *Vivement la solitude (Bring on Solitude)*. The therapist does not get tangled into the *folds* of the other person but locates herself *in the folds of the relationship.*

For the therapist, differentiation allows her to be fully present without being *infected* by the problems or the emotional state of the person who comes in consultation. She doesn't have any need to withdraw or intervene to defend her own emotional state. For example, if the person is sad, his sadness is deeply felt not just seen. Then the therapist takes note mentally of the sadness, very simply, without reaction, without taking any action. That emotion must be held from a state of love.

Differentiation promotes the evolution of the skill of feeling separate in therapy and also in an intimate relationship. It's an attitude of non-reactivity to the reactions of the client—done out of respect, non-judgment and thoughtfulness. Empathy is necessary not symbiosis or personal power. The heart is present accompanying the process of thought.

Having understood and integrated these essential elements of the therapeutic relationship ensures a better practice of trance work. I will come back to this when we come to look more deeply at ethics in the therapeutic process as it relates to channeling in the first annex.

All inner work, whether it is accomplished within the framework of psychotherapy, body work, or energy work, allows a definite movement toward oneself and toward spiritual awakening. For myself, years of work of all kinds led me to osteopathy. This approach harvested all that had been sown by each of the previous approaches and allowed my body, and therefore my life, to really liberate itself from the past and to experience a long-awaited flowering. I have never been as supple, healthy and serene as I am now. That's how it was for me. Perhaps having a massage once a week or consulting a homeopath will lead you to more happiness. It could also result from beginning to run, to dance, taking up yoga or even entrusting your body to allopathic medicine following a serious illness or an accident. The choice doesn't matter provided that you don't stop once you've begun. Because healing love increases with each step forward...

Meditating in the Inner World's Light

Walking through and moving forward in the physical leads to contemplation of the beauty of the visible world. Meditation, another aspect of the spiritual journey, leads to contemplation of the inner world's light.

As the years flowed by, I meditated—in groups or alone, lying down, sitting, standing, being motionless as much as possible or walking, in a more or less regular way, more or less disciplined. I practiced this art for better or for worse, more worse than better, feeling an obligation, like a religious duty, not like a divine quest or a feast. I practiced it without joy. All knowing related to meditation therefore remained theoretical. I only knew intellectually the benefits of this exercise that I wasn't able to master. Nobody had told me that meditation could be pleasurable and that, for some people, it is useless to practice it as a discipline.

I remember that after having read a text from the Old or New Testament, the nuns in my primary school said they meditated on it. They meant that they had *reflected* on what they had read. I don't believe they had ever had the Church's permission to do anything other than reflect and come to the same conclusions as those of the religious authorities. Creativity and freedom of thought get initiated in the body. They had no right to live in a nun's sinful body. No more than is the case for their male counterparts I might say. In monasteries however, meditation perhaps became real prayer. Material obligations and preoccupations were reduced and worldly distractions were excluded. Prayer had a chance to be more sincere, the return to the center of oneself and to the innocence of childhood was more assured, and being present to the body more affirmed. Perhaps that's how it was for some men and women. In her autobiography, Teresa of Ávila describes her meditations this way: "Quietude and contemplation are things that the soul feels deeply through the satisfaction and peace that it enjoys. The soul is then in possession, at one and the same time, of a very great contentment, a resting from its powers and a very sweet pleasure." This pleasure, as we can understand from the description of her ecstasies, she felt deeply, sensitively and physically.

> In an era that honors pay-back, efficiency and combat, it is essential to foster a return to our inner being. This dimension is nourished by providing oneself with times of silence, non-willing and non-doing.
> Jean Marie Dillemain

Meditating—a Joyful Wandering

Meditation is allowing oneself to glide from the left hemisphere of the brain toward the right hemisphere, from agitation of thought to its absence, from the condensed to the expanded and all of this without an aim. It is a joyful wandering without trying to establish a specific communication with the invisible—some might say with God. It involves establishing a close contact with your body and your breathing, with the vibration of the body—a more or less strong one—but vibration just the same. In the attention brought to this light oscillation, to this faint trembling as a tantric practitioner would say, breathing reveals its sweetness. It begins to feel good and that is why the desire to return to it takes up residence in oneself and allows a coming back to the body. Coming back to oneself is first of all inhabiting one's body and one's sensory faculties.

To get to that point, you need to be capable of taming not only thoughts, but also emotions, without denying them, without trying to get rid of them; they will find places for themselves where they are most helpful. You need to know how to let yourself surf along the wave of each emotion and ride it right to the end, managing to prolong the last movement of the undulation as long as possible. Until the next swell of emotions or the next invasion of thoughts. There is a time for the rational and for the emotional and there is a time for their opposites— this taste for a pause, for peace, for the pleasure of being there, simply, very simply just there. There is a time for contemplation, for gathering oneself together in meditation, for doing it once again and completely. Or even harvesting the richness of certain emotions. Meditating *within* sadness, for example. Why not? Contemplating your anger or your fear without resistance, letting yourself move through them, flow through their generous matrices, letting yourself be marked with their imprints, why not? Consciousness of the present doesn't imply changing what is, but rather exploring all its nuances. Practice a hunkering down that is unconditional and, if necessary, egoistic. This means without waiting for the dissolution of the ego, without wanting silence at any price, without looking for it, without forcing it, just waiting for it, just being there, in presence— and if that means being present to inner tumult, so be it!

When younger, coming to the Light's remarkable and welcoming peace seemed to me to represent an arduous and boring work. But the divine is essentially joyous. We cannot imagine the divine leaning with all seriousness into its worktable, eyebrows clenched and forehead determined. We cannot imagine a God who is depressed, negative or even emotional. Emotion is human because it is an energy in movement in the body. God, or Life if you prefer, is love, pure love. He is easily love because He does not languish in physical density. But we, we must embrace our emotions (or even set them alight!) in order to fully experience our humanity and to rise up from our humanity. No one had told me that the peace that comes during meditation tastes good, that this taste is one of joy, and that that kind of joy is not an emotion. Joy is the radiating color of love and love is not established through work or discipline. Love in its joyful quintessence is chosen and is won through the healing of emotional wounds that mark the body. Joy is born in a clear, open body...

Meditating in Feminine or in Masculine Ways

Paths to access the divine are multiple and changing. Mysterious, complex or simplistic, they are imposed on our attention with insistence even when it's in an elusive way. Moreover, they have gender—masculine or feminine.

Masculine meditation, practiced by women as well as men, calls for more discipline, more regularity and more rigor both in its form and in its frequency. It conforms to strict rules. Huston Smith, author of *The World's Religions*, tells how he spent time in a monastery in Asia and how he was able to be initiated there into Buddhism on the condition that he succeed in sitting in lotus position during long hours of meditation. He did succeed. He reports that, during the first two months, every day, the long, extremely long, duration of the sitting created an atrocious pain of unbearable intensity, but he continued his training through sheer will power. In order to do this, he had to keep his body erect, silence its complaint and ignore his suffering.

This is a masculine approach and is valid for some people and at certain specific times. However, it is possible to move upward spiritually in a more feminine way; this is possible for men just as for women. A gentler and yet just as effective practice of meditation is to be found in Daniel Odier's way of practicing and teaching Kashmiri tantric texts. This involves micro-meditations within the banality of everyday life, the eyes remaining wide open to reality.

In an interview conducted by Anne Devillard, Odier suggests "daily reality as a field of practice, without giving up anything at all, simply being completely in contact with the world." Each movement of life in oneself, in the body or in the emotions, is observed without judgment; more than observed, it is experienced to the full. Automatisms are recognized as such and are set aside in order to prefer a fully-conscious and agreed-upon contact with reality. Odier tells us, "In order to reach this profound presence, it is essential that this marvelous instrument that is our body be perfectly attuned. This is where sense impressions come into the picture. The first stage then is to restore all these functions, to rediscover our taste for life, to be totally available to life with all our senses, our desires and our passions."

The way of simplicity and the way of the body open with ease in quite brief meditations where the heart can rightfully sing, raise the tone or murmur its song, where the body is no longer tortured, rejected or hated but is honored.

It is important for the channeler to ceaseless attune himself to daily life.

> *Facing up to the adversity and fragility of life bothers me. Arising from this omnipresent difficulty, a desire for unity, transcendence, lightness and the infinite has sprouted in me. In a search for balance, the thickness of my life is pushing me to want to penetrate the light and blend with it. To want to leave suffering behind,*

to cast off my leaden mantle, for a moment that is blessed, for an intermediary, for a breathing out before the next breathing in. Patiently, I seek to manifest this quintessence which insists on escaping from my daily life. I seek to integrate these opposites, to dissolve all tensions that result from being attached to a vibration of humanity. I am a human who embraces the subtle, who sighs following effort... and who, in the reality of things, valiantly undertakes once again the next in-breath.

I frequently travel from my head to my sex, to my body, to my life, to my head. A thousand times a day, I bring myself back to the present, to the pleasure of feeling well in my body, in my skin, in my senses, here and now. I stop. I make contact again. I escape and I come back. I wander away and I always come home again. The road is longer, less long, harder, less hard, but the coming home... Ah! The coming home...
Passages from my diary

Channeling: Touching Divine Light

I firmly believe that intuitive or symbolic sight is not a gift but a skill—a skill based in self-esteem. Developing this skill—and a healthy sense of self—becomes easier when you can think in the words, concepts, and principles of energy medicine—think of learning to use intuition as learning to interpret the language of energy.
Caroline Myss

The channeler enters into trance and opens herself to a communication with Light Beings whether their energy is angelic, Christ-like, Pleiadian or some other energy.

As for the spirit medium, she enters into trance, induces an altered state in herself, and contacts deceased persons who live in the astral world. This invisible world exists in a parallel dimension, a kind of subtle location consisting of paradise, purgatory and possibly hell, which shelters souls in transit between two lives. According to their degree of evolution and the acceptance or rejection of this transiting that has to be experienced, those souls will have the impression of living either in heaven or in hell. Paradise or hell are not locations, they are states that are experienced on earth and can be reproduced in the other world. In the astral, between two lives on earth, souls sometimes experience confusion or blindness. They need help. If they have found out how to adapt, they will be much more capable of offering their support to those who are still in the human dimension. Entering into contact with them is beneficial. It can be an asset in personal and spiritual development.

The clairvoyant recognizes the presence of a higher vibration but speaks from her own intuition while her state is more or less altered.

The meditator seeks to empty his mind, to welcome the silence, to explore unity in himself and unity with what is. According to the type of meditation being practiced, the bodily felt sense is either probed or denied.

For the channeler, the medium or the clairvoyant, the emptiness leads to an *activity from the heart*, and to offering intuitive and loving words (or a gesture). The client and his specificity are welcomed with the felt sense of the body and of the emotions not with the intellect. This receptivity in facing the human side of life strengthens the link with the divine and allows a contact with its light.

In meditation and in channeling, calming down the body and having it fully present is not just favorable, it is required. *You descend down into the body.* In trance, a conscious modification of the energy frequency is necessary. Whereas in meditation, there is no longer anything *to do.*

Using your intuition is one of the elements of trance work. Giving yourself over to the luminous energy is another. Being present to the person to whom you are transmitting a message is essential in order to feel that person's energy and to penetrate its subtlety in order to be able to read it. This art of presence cannot be practiced without an integration of the personality through constant inner work.

> "Bring your awareness to your base energy center. This spot is charged with love and will allow you to reconnect with the mother-aspect that desires you. Because even if you did not deeply feel the desire of your physical mother for you, your spiritual mother, in contrast, from her great goodness, wanted you to be on earth. This desire, coming from Mother-Earth, this desire for life for you—you must find it again. And make it your own.
>
> There is a form of quietening that is going to spread little by little through the channel of the heart. It is connected to a fullness in the body. It won't be the intellect that is going to offer you a way out. Nourish yourself by what you feel deeply in your body. Don't hurry. Take your time." *Message from Guides*

— Reflection—

Know Yourself and Meditate

Are you well acquainted with the story of your life? Can you recount it clearly and emphasize its redeeming message?

Are you still harboring certain grudges? Are you up-to-date emotionally? Are you well acquainted with yourself on this plane?

Are you well acquainted with your body, with its sensory faculties and its sexuality?

Is your material life in order? Are your finances and your professional life in order?

What are the values that you promote in your personal life? In your professional life? In your trance work?

You have difficulty meditating? Daniel Odier, in an interview with Anne Devillard, suggests micro-meditations inspired by tantric masters. It involves coming to total presence for a few seconds at a time. Yes, just a few seconds at a time...

> "The idea behind micro-meditations is to have your system re-encounter the evidence that presence brings you more joy than your automatism does. It's as simple as that. So, if you have your system taste something delicious for 10 or 15 seconds and then you leave it alone and then you have it taste it again there will be a moment when your system will desire it. It comes by itself. This is what's so strong about the micro-meditations. You do them for two or three months, and suddenly, life comes looking for you and says, 'OK then, stay with me for 20 seconds! You feel the call of things, you come back, you stay there and then you let go'."
> Daniel Odier

Chapter 7

Protecting

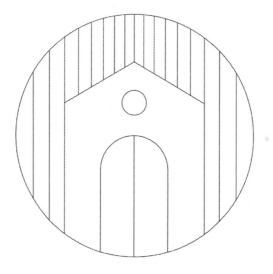

Psychic self-protection consists of creating a secure space in which to live, work and exist. It creates healthy limits and a calm, quiet center in which you can just be.
Judy Hall

Thinking about Your Need for Protection

Your ability to protect yourself psychically during trance work is proportional to your ability to protect yourself in the everyday world.

If you improve your clarity in one, the other will profit from it. If you know how to protect yourself, those consulting you will be protected as well. In any therapeutic profession or in your life, you need to situate yourself in relation to your own system of beliefs and values. This is one of the best protections.

Light workers, who are you? What is the specific nature of your trances? What is the state of your electromagnetic field? What is the condition of your nervous system? What in particular frightens you? How do you care for your beliefs, for yourself, for your heart, for your emotions? In relating to the invisible world, do you cultivate fears or instead a feeling of security? Do you feel accompanied by positive energies? Do you know how to call them; do you want to call them? What protection in particular do you need in each domain of your life?

Why Protect Yourself during Trance Work?

Don't protect yourself out of fear. Not because of any particular danger. The creation of a ritualized physical perimeter of protection is one element that ensures effective trance work. This workspace is a sacred construct in which the channeler feels securely held by the environment allowing the message to unfold in a more authentic manner.

Imagine being at home in the evening. You are getting ready to go to bed. You take a shower or a bath, you brush your teeth.

Then, you walk through the house. You verify that everything is ready for the night: Heat or light sources (candles, lamps, stove elements) are turned off. Doors are carefully locked. You make sure that everything is cleaned up, closed or opened, placed or replaced, prepared for the next day. You conduct the evening ritual and you know you will sleep better. If you do this absent-mindedly, without being present to your usual movements, you have trouble getting to sleep. You will have to get up: "Did I really lock the front door?" You check, you discover that you did, you go back to bed and you fall asleep. This ritual is not carried out because you are really afraid of thieves. It is conducted because it reassures you, because it gives you a framework and allows you to sleep. Also, because it's good to be careful. However, there is no imminent danger. And there isn't any in trance work either.

An Arab proverb says, "Trust God but tether your camel." It's of no help to be afraid. You have to act—but with care and ritually. The protection ritual to be conducted for trance work has certain similarities to the nighttime ritual in that it sees to a cleansing of oneself and of the area, to a quietening of thought, and to the installation of some protection parameters. If you are watchful in protecting yourself during the trance, the person consulting you will also be protected.

Feeling Safe

With respect to trance work, the best protection available, besides clarity in relation to your values and beliefs, is work on yourself and grounding.

Self-knowledge is a much more reliable measure of success than knowledge of techniques or the practice of certain exercises. Techniques and exercises are necessary but they will never replace an enlightened consciousness and an inner wisdom, especially when cultivated at higher frequencies. Inner work and grounding ensure the vitality of the aura by sustaining its vibratory rhythm. In *Psychic Protection,* Ted Andrews affirms that a strong and vibrant aura sheds negative, unbalanced energies that deplete our life energy. He suggests ways of helping to vivify the aura or the electromagnetic field: sensible exposure to solar energy, fresh, non-polluted air, and physical exercise. Eating smaller portions more frequently is often good for the health of the aura. Intestines that work well too. He advises meditation. I would add prayer and *unencumbered* thought.

Rest for the body and the digestive system maintains the health of the nervous system. Actions that are integrated and grounded are less at risk of being invaded by negative energies whether they be human or astral. What surrounds us, just as what constitutes our inner environment, has a certain impact on our feeling of security.

A myth to unravel: The invisible seems so much stronger and more powerful than us. A noise from an unknown cause frightens us more than a noise we know. The unknown we call cancer seems deadly whereas cancerous cells are in fact confused cells that have lost their sense of direction. Beings from the low astral region are desperate and confused beings who have lost the meaning of their death; they are subtle cancerous cells who no longer know which way is up. They attack fragile personalities. If we are fully aware of our strength and our integrity, we become invulnerable to these misplaced forces. As for the greats of black magic, they are not interested in us. I believe that our meditations, our prayers, our positive intentions, our work of mental and subtle detoxification short circuit their direct action if there would be one.

Protecting Yourself and Those Who Consult You—but from What?

What's the worst thing that can happen? A psychic attack from detractors? An invasion by negative energy? Possession by a spirit from the low astral region? What else? What are you afraid of?

Knowing what we are afraid of is the best way to resolve our fears. Without unreasonable fears, real dangers can be faced better because our strength is intact—it is not depleted by a feeling that has no roots in reality.

The world is our own creation. Our thoughts, our beliefs and our actions fashion our immediate world and the entire universe. Yes, me, this *little nothing me* creates the energy of the world... I do my part. Do I decide to do good or not so good? My little *I* is like a drop of water in the ocean—but a real and essential one.

Protecting ourselves from others is a phony concept. We are not in danger from others; we are in danger from ourselves. Our thoughts are our worst enemy. Too many thoughts, confused, exacerbated, negatively-oriented thoughts take us away from our center, the place where we are sheltered from everything! Do I exaggerate? Perhaps... What do you think?

On the other hand, periods of great vulnerability can occur— after an illness, your own or that of someone you love, at the time of a burnout or life crisis, during periods of great stress whatever its cause might be. Here are a few indicators that help identify when our defenses have become less effective:

1. Dreams change and become nightmares peopled by the same characters. Disagreeable situations keep repeating. In fact, the unconscious is trying to send alarm signals. Look for the underlying cause of these nightmares. I am not referring here to childhood nightmares, but those that appear in our adult life and which repeat—without our consent. I affirm that we will always be victorious in our own world when we are acutely aware of who we are.

2. Anxiety which manifests more as a weight on the chest than as a tightening.

3. New fears and obsessions that are not let go of easily.

4. Nervous system fatigue.

5. Inexplicable bad smells around you.

6. Increasingly great discomfort around certain people or certain locations.

7. Insomnia that has no apparent cause.

8. Electrical problems in the home.

9. Temperature changes and inexplicable phenomena around you.

10. Great tiredness when around certain people.

Becoming aware of what is happening and taking concrete action are the first steps toward a solution.

How to Know if You Are in Danger

High-level guides neither frighten you nor lord it over you. They support and encourage you to develop and use your inner strengths and deeper wisdom.
Sanaya Roman and Duane Packer

The Guides and the channeler have to work in harmony. If the voice of the person you consult is hard, authoritarian and doesn't sound good to you, it could be that this person is working from her ego or that her Guides are not very elevated. Authenticity is something you feel, something you pick up on. Are you really able to tell with whom you are dealing? Are you someone who often *falls in* with people who don't seem to project positive energies toward others? Examining yourself carefully is appropriate in this regard. Can you identify in yourself the faculty of perception that allows you to create a safe and healthy environment?

Our body responds to truth. We need to pay attention to its messages.

High Guides help us to develop a more enlightened awareness and a broader, breathing inner vision that nourishes those around us. They encourage us to stay close to our center and not to blindly follow directives coming from an energy that wants to hold power over us. They also protect us from less positive energies. Being loving, they don't try to take power over us, they don't tell us what to do, they send us back to ourselves, enlightened, stronger, and richer.

Those who consult medium and channeler ought to feel comforted by the movement of Higher Energies through their lives. If you are the practitioner, you should feel good after delivering a message. Joy should be present in this work. If not, you should be asking yourself questions. Feeling a little tired is normal. Needing to take care of one's liver and one's health in general goes without saying. But if you are feeling sad or depressed, you need to ask yourself two questions: What are my motivations in doing this work? Who is coming through me? It's very likely that the first question is more important than the second. You need to ask who you are channeling. The astral is that world of the soul that is called the other world. Several levels of different vibrations are to be found there which shelter souls at certain moments of their life-after-death, based on their level of development. The astral is often divided into three parts: The upper astral, the middle astral and the lower astral. Each level is formed from a collection of thought forms (an egregoir) that belongs to a degree of evolution, and each level represents a world in itself corresponding to a time period in the life of the soul. The intention in channeling is to reach or to let oneself be reached by Light Beings—Guides who have attained a more pure state and who have left the astral behind.

Create a Secure Container for Your Work

Do your trance work in a place you love. Where beauty joins the session. Where symbols used with discretion and simplicity make you feel good.

1. Symbols

Inspiring, uplifting images. Vertical images. Trees are excellent. They rise up, spread out into space, rooting themselves at the same time. Avoid images that directly refer to religious dogma. Garlic is a protector. Place some in a little bowl and replace it every week.

2. Colors

Colors in your surroundings must go with the color of your skin. And the color of your aura. Colors that make your aura sparkle, that awaken it. Colors that *enchant* you. Think of your chakras when you choose colors for your workplace. For example, mauve is often used because it is associated with the third eye, but do you really need it right now? If you need grounding, place a few red objects or red splashes in your sanctuary. Not too many because in excess red produces the opposite effect. If you want your professional work to expand, use yellow, a bright yellow. If you want to express yourself with more precision, use blue. And so on. As you know, the choice of colors that are around you is not without effect.

3. Stones, Crystals, Salts and Herbs

Epsom salt and sea salt are known to be purifying and protective. Formerly, they were spread on the thresholds of homes to keep undesirable visitors at a distance. Place salt or a bowl of salt water in your workplace. Put Epsom salt in your evening bath. Bathe in the sea as often as possible.

Stones are living beings, aware and stable. They know how to inspire you in the transmission of your message of light. Their presence reminds you of the necessity of staying grounded.

Crystals: all those you have been called to and have bought intuitively or received as gifts. Amethyst and quartz are the best protectors.

Sage: smudge your workspace with sage at regular intervals.

4. Odors

Essential lavender oil is restful, promotes sleep and lucid dreams. Trance is a little like a lucid dream. Essential oil of hemlock opens the throat chakra in order to provide more articulate messages. Choose very gentle incense because the odor can be invasive. *Dragon's blood* incense attracts higher energies while driving away lower level energies. Sage is very purifying.

In Summary:

For Better Protection

- Carefully define your work and its specific characteristics

- Set up a trance ritual. In other words, create an effective and safe container for the energy that is mobilized during a channeling.

- Foster good health in the nervous system

- Ensure your grounding in day-to-day life.

- Look after your health in general. Subtle energies are managed by the liver more than any other organ. The liver must continue to be able to sustain this additional work as must the body as a whole.

- Cultivate a strong and vibrant aura.

- Always continue introspection, work on yourself.

Chapter 8

Channeling

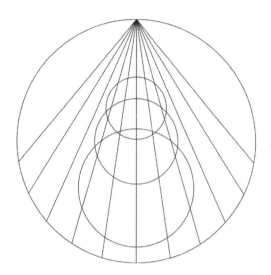

...I define the shaman (man or woman) as a healer of relationships: relationships between the body and soul, between people, between beings and circumstances, between humans and nature, between spirit and matter. The nature of shamanism is such that you heal yourself in healing others and you transform yourself in transforming the planet.
Serge Kahili King

Receiving and Transmitting

How could we think of healing small parts of one's life without taking into account life as a whole?

Regardless of the tradition to which a healer belongs, the objectives defined by Serge Kahili King at the beginning of this chapter are a very tall order! In fact, the whole life in all its aspects is held, symbolically, in the hands of the channeler, the medium or the shaman. They must be loving without being complacent, and firm without being invasive. The appropriateness of the practitioner's support is proportional to the authenticity of his work on himself. In this context, the word *shaman* must be considered in the broader meaning of a light worker—only the manner differs. The range of communication with the world above and with the Higher Self is vast and various. Modified states of consciousness develop in several ways and have rather different goals. Here are just some of them:

The **shamanic trance** and the **ritualistic trance** involve healing work as in channeling but follow a different modality. These trances are induced using the entrancing rhythms of drumming and very energetic, even frenetic, dances. Masks are sometimes used to invite certain qualities and to invoke other forms. In the ritualistic trance, the healer can have recourse to sounds, cries, songs, rhythms, or theater in order to induce and deepen the trance. All the chakras are open but it is the energy of the eighth chakra that does the healing work.

The **psychedelic trance** is induced by hallucinogenic substances and can allow a certain personal and spiritual development. Hypnotic trance, mystical ecstasy, sexual ecstasy, the ecstasy of creation and enlightenment all pursue the same evolutionary aims. The trance provoked by turning dance such as that practiced by the whirling dervishes follows these aims as well.

The **mediumistic trance** and **channeling** support the personal and spiritual development of the person practicing them and they lead those who consult to evolve toward greater awareness of themselves and of their Higher Selves—on condition, of course, that they consciously desire that evolution. Healing of the heart through compassion and letting go is fostered by these two approaches. The state of trance is induced by calm, presence to the body, breathing, and visualization. In channeling, the state of trance can be deep or light, modulated or refined, conscious or less conscious. In very rare cases there is incorporation meaning that the individual in trance allows himself to be almost completely penetrated by an Entity of Light. However, this is never complete; the consciousness of the medium-in-trance is always present in part. I have chosen to practice and teach deep conscious trance. I don't believe that there are trances where the human consciousness disappears completely. There are trances that are deeper or purer, but our human observation process continues to make a selection of what is seen and transmitted.

How?

The ways of managing to induce a deep conscious trance are many but certain ones are essential: Presence to the body, special breathing and the penetration of certain images.

An enhanced **presence of the physical body** supports the withdrawal of the ego and sometimes even the total absence of bodily demarcations or borders. In our *waking state*, our ordinary/ day-to-day state, awareness of the body is sometimes diffuse or scattered or can also be magnified if identification with the body and its sense perceptions is almost total. The modified state of consciousness suspends identification of the self with the body during the time of the trance. What ensues is a greater contact with bodily experience, since the ego creates no interference. The person becomes an observer of his body as if the body were an entity in its own right; the body is both someone else and oneself at the same time. In order to come to the vibrational essence of the body, which is dense by nature, you need first of all to be fully aware of the relationship that is maintained with the body and with the image of the body. In other words, it is due to the love of your body that its vibrations are sufficiently attuned so that it can enter into a higher frequency of energy. The person in trance, through a body that she is not identified with but is vibrating at a higher rate, can come into attunement with both the dense reality and subtle reality of the client. The body becomes the kernel that the consciousness relies on to experience an expansion in space and to make contact with the other person and the invisible Guides.

Fast breathing (panting or jerky) or **slowed breathing** (deep and slow) are other ways of deliberately creating a trance. Breathing by filling the central channel is another. Circular breathing (see end of chapter) prepares one for the practice of these specific breathing modalities by releasing cellular memory which slows down the action of breathing.

A trance can be induced by a specific **visualization**. For example: wandering in the heart of nature, meeting a wise old man in a given place in your inner world, gliding through a bottomless ocean, imagining a mass of information organized into a virtual library and choosing to access some of it. It's not just a matter of seeing the image but more importantly of allowing it to pervade you or going with it completely.

Several scenarios of life itself spontaneously lead to states of trance or modified consciousness: An intense fatigue, physical or psychological trauma, very high fever, oceanic feelings created by orgasm, sensory deprivation, hyper stimulation of the imagination (as in artistic creation), lengthy or often repeated prayer or meditation, for example. These trances are real but *unintentional*. They are not designed to help someone else.

Intention

The state of trance is defined by an intention that it is based on. The shaman wants to heal, the tripper wants to escape and enjoy, the meditator wants to awaken, the yogi wants to stay in contact with the divine, the medium wants to receive messages from deceased persons, the channeler enters into communication with Light Beings or Guides and wants to be of service to humanity by giving messages that are helpful, elevated and elevating. In these cases, everyone is searching for spiritual development and for the meaning of life—even in the case of trances induced by addictive substances. And finally, everyone is seeking to tap into their innate healing power even if confusion hinders this effort in the case of those dependent on substances like alcohol, drugs, food, or frantic activities like extreme sports or hyper-sexuality.

Trance work in all its forms is more than a state of trance. It is an art and an involvement in the service of humanity—without being self-serving. It participates in the awakening of higher consciousness in the world. Each chakra must be harmonized with the totality of the personality so that one or several psychic abilities enjoy significant development. In return, all developmental movements of these talents, whether they be innate or acquired, harmonize the corresponding chakra.

Trance work participates in the awakening of a higher consciousness in the world.

Relevance to the State of Trance

Man must be able to bring forward proof that he has done everything possible to form a conception or an image of life after death even when that would be an admission of his powerlessness. He who has not done this suffers a loss. Because the interrogative imperative that holds forth in him is a very ancient inheritance of humanity—it is an archetype, rich with a secret life that wants to join with our life in order to perfect it. Reason imposes much too narrow limits and invites us to experience only what is known (and even that with many restrictions) and to experience it in a known framework, as if we knew the true extent of life. In fact, our life, day after day, goes far beyond the limits of our consciousness and without our knowing it, the life of the unconscious accompanies our existence. The more critical reason predominates, the more impoverished our life becomes. However, the more we are able to make conscious what is unconscious and what is myth, the greater is the amount of life that we integrate into ourselves. Over-valuing reason has this in common with the power of dictatorship: Under its domination, the individual wastes away.
C.G. Jung

Why is spirituality looked on in such a bad light? Why is it that confusion between the words religious and spiritual continues to exist? Why doesn't intuition and its many benefits have any place in education? Why would a psychologist be less competent if he were to develop his intuition and place it at the service of his technical skills?

In a recent psychology congress, it was said that Quebec psychologists should beware of *charlatans* who use intuitive ways of working. In fact, mediums were specifically mentioned and they were all put in the same bag without distinction—conscientious light workers thrown together with those who lack professionalism. Mediumship and its whole range of modalities are looked upon badly because they are not always practiced as an art that creates an opening in the client. They do not ensure that he is led into self-examination without being taken over and without power-plays (we might ask, in passing, if the science of psychology itself is conducted without power issues). Divinatory arts are often practiced without respect for therapeutic boundaries and without professional ethics—and sometimes with an attitude of imposing control. In fact, this is done in medicine as well as in psychology and religion. There are good physicians, good psychologists and good priests and some who are not so good. There are light workers who are not so good. However, certain of them really place themselves at the service of their fellow human beings and the Earth while others work for themselves. Being watchful about the quality of any intuitive work is a goal that I aspire to throughout this book.

As Jung stresses, life deserves to be lived in its entirety while being aware that mistakes can be made but also being clear that dismissing a whole level of reality is, in itself, a serious mistake.

Listening

I listen to others with total presence. My whole body listens and, beyond language, I understand what the bodies tell me.
Daniel Odier

Knowing how to listen to what life has to say, through intuition, with the help of the presence of Light Beings or souls of the deceased, or simply with the help of a deep listening to oneself, demands a highly developed aptitude for entering into silence, for experiencing all the creative power of welcoming in, and for giving oneself over to what is. There is listening to the vibration of the other person and there is listening to Guides. This is what I call sacred listening and it must go in two directions: Towards the human and towards the divine.

Offering a Channeling Session

Even though the process is specific, the result is diversified and unexpected—It is not about looking for a result.

The quality of the message depends on the channeler and on his client. It is good not to have any expectation, any pre-judgment and to demystify the phenomenon. The message comes from a Higher Source but the channeler remains human. The channeling is a collaboration between the two. This Higher Source can be felt as a luminous vibration or as the inner place that is sometimes called the Self. In either case, if the message is given with love and with the intention of being of service to the person who comes for a consultation, its help is precious.

When I receive a person for channeling, I enter a state of prayer. I give thanks for the opportunity that I have been given to serve humanity. I am always guided by an intention of service. I create a bubble of protection around myself by imagining sea salt thrown in the four directions: In front of me and behind me, to my left and to my right. I call upon benevolent Light Beings thanking them for their presence. I send others who might appear back to their worlds telling them they are not welcome. This is a necessary precaution, not a necessity, because dark beings do not appear in a place where the trance has been ritualized or with a person whose energy bodies are whole.

I visualize myself in nature. Through breathing, I calm my mind, I slow my thoughts, I let go of them almost completely, I descend into my body, my energetic frequency rises. My subtle body expands and begins to join the subtle body of my client. The presence of my Guides becomes almost tangible. They have lowered their vibratory frequency and they meet me at the level I try to raise myself to. They call out to me in this energetic location. I thank them for being in contact with me and for accepting to help the person who is consulting me. An emotional state, impressions, physical sensations arise and become more precise all during the meeting. Sometimes words move in. Distinct images with bright colors and nuances appear. Even though they are static at first, they will be in constant movement all the time I'm describing them. Each detail, each color, each movement reveals its secret drop by drop. I watch the images dancing behind my closed eyelids. I let them be. They begin to talk.

The light absorbs me completely: It takes me, it holds me and it keeps me from fleeing. I extend myself toward the other person, my state of consciousness enlarges, the right hemisphere of my brain *lights up*.

Transmitting: Giving a Helpful Message

A message begins to take shape. I let myself drift into a first thought or a first image. I abandon myself to a different energy. I'm never afraid. I experience an ever-changing trance. It deepens, lightens, deepens again depending on the resistance or the acceptance of the other person, and depending on my ability at the moment to resist all distraction. I remain present, receptive and almost asleep, but conscious just the same. If the message no longer conforms to my values I would intervene and say no to this or that. My values, being clearly identified, ensure my *centering*. For example, I don't make any predictions. I don't announce anyone's death or I never say to leave a partner or cut ties with a friend or relative, unless it's just for a short time. The deep, conscious trance has the advantage of protecting the free will of the person-in-trance. I use *we* to mean that my Guides and I speak in mutual agreement.

If the person who is consulting me is open, I feel received, welcomed. Otherwise I don't abandon the person to her resistance but I stay respectfully at the threshold of her doorway accepting that she may not open the door. I knock, I begin to chat through the closed door. Being less fearful, the person opens the door a crack or sometimes completely—or halfway.

I descend into my heart. I visualize it in the process of opening. Drunvalo Melchizedek in the book *Living in the Heart*, affirms that you need only turn the inner eye toward the physical heart and watch it in order to be in your energetic heart. I know this experience well.

Love is a state of vibration. I have learned to create it in myself at will. Love for the person in front of me, for my work, for the Light. Love inhabits me and my Guides follow its vibration. They play the instrument that I become for a moment. I try to play this music with Them as best I can by bringing in all possible subtleties in reaching my client. The person feels something very comforting, very real, beyond the words, through the words. A number of people cry all through the message without knowing why.

A page of their current life is being read. The reading proposes spiritual and human outcomes that must be seen as possibilities, not certainties. The subtle link between the present and a potentiality in the future is being illuminated. The channeling facilitates the ordering of solutions already known but misunderstood by the client. For example, a woman wants to know if she will have children. The energy is scanned, the body appears in its subtle form, her aura reveals areas that are dark or fully illuminated. The body can create a child—everything is there, all is in order. Perhaps there are even souls who are standing right beside the soul of the person who is asking the question. Everything is there. But, the next morning, this woman can get up and decide to never have children. The message does not present a promise, a prediction or an obligation. The free will of the person coming for a consultation is still in place. Simply put, she was able to be informed about the possibility of having a child and about the non-medical path (the reading of the subtle energy does not replace official fertility tests) that she can follow to achieve that goal.

In other words, a channeling, or reading of the subtle energy, is a meditation open to Love that brings the client back to her own intuition, to her creativity and to her intimate divinity. Channeling is a ministry of love and the heart is its sanctuary.

During a channeling then, I enter into a deep, conscious trance. I work in concert with the Energies of the Christ-Light who come forward under the name of Joshua and are accompanied by two or three other luminous energies, also of a Christ-like nature. A channeling is similar to a conference call. I remain present while at the same time making myself available to this

Higher Self which is a channel for listening to the other world and which is attuned to Unity. The Christ-Energies inspire me, presenting me with their knowledge and their words in this work of accompaniment and spiritual guidance.

I always continue the work of grounding and of accepting my human nature. In order to become a helpful channel it is necessary first and foremost that I purify my observation of myself and of life so that the seeing of the subtle energy remains healthy—I could say holy—expanded and vivifying. We must also admit that we will make errors and we need to say so. We should not imply that our messages are perfect and that they contain no subjectivity or distortion.

Completing the Meeting

I briefly offer, if possible and desirable, a summarized reformulation of the principal points of the meeting repeating one or two areas to be worked on. Example: "It seems to me that my Guides are sending you a message to work on the body at this time in your life and in the given situation."

I encourage the person to take responsibility. I help them identify their needs and the totality of their experience in relation to the meeting—always briefly so it doesn't become too rational—and only if appropriate.

I stay very close to the essence of the message and avoid talking about it too much. I shun an excess of words and explanations. I do not respond to any additional questions (which could have been forgotten by the recipient during the trance) except those which connect to the unfolding of the meeting which is ending. I must accept right away that the person will either be satisfied or not satisfied with their consultation.

Energetic Balance in Channeling

The consciousness is receptive and is directed toward *open space* and upward (yin aspect) from a firm base, from a robust support structure (yang aspect) connected into our deepest roots. This anchor point must remain *illuminated* all during the transmission of a message (yang aspect). For some individuals, this connection point could be a *trance director* (a person who accompanies the channeler and induces the trance). I have chosen not to work with a trance director in order to ensure greater discretion for those who consult me.

The consciousness travels through the chakras which open fully in all directions and well beyond the physical body. The essential fuel necessary for this ascension, this expedition, is the fundamental vitality which is also sexual energy. This is why it is important to keep sexual energy really vibrant in daily life.

Consciousness deepens and expands at the same time (yin/yang). Thoughts become quiet; the body becomes calm. Presence to oneself is total; nothing is dampened down. A canvas appears— pristine and full at the same time, ready to be repainted. Everything goes into the formation of a message: An itchy foot, discomfort in the stomach, distractions, sounds from outside, changing light behind the closed eyelids, words that you hear in the back of your head, the quivering of the eyelids and other parts of the body, images that appear, you notice their movement, their colors, you pay attention to words that get caught in your throat, coughing that seems to be yours but belongs to the other person. You resist nothing, and everything is welcomed. **You don't just empty your mind, you fill up your heart.**

Channeling: an Energy Exchange

In channeling, the heart reaches out, the mind distances itself, or sometimes becomes completely silent. You become *enfolded*. You lose yourself in the *folds* of the other person as the vibratory state rises. There is no anxiety. This isn't a symbiosis however. **It's an opening to unity, a work of pacification, a recognition of non-separation with all that is.** Allowing a penetration by the Light, the human and the divine search each other out in greater depth. As if each person were embraced by this new frequency that becomes established and is *breathed in*. Each channeling is a revelation rather than a message, a spiritual healing rather than advice to be taken even if advice is given. One day, I really think that there will no longer be words in my readings as support for the energy of the heart, but only the establishment in the silence of an inspiring and therefore healing vibratory frequency. I am presently exploring this way of working and the results are good but not yet conclusive enough to offer it exclusively.

I love the image of a tree: Well rooted, all branches out and up, the tree buries itself in the earth at the same time that it totally projects its branches outward. The roots are as deep as the branches are high. The branches extend just as far in all directions as do the roots. The sap is the essential fuel that is nourished by the earth, providing back to the earth in exchange a refined vibration, and, with the same impulse, nourishing the tree branches that reach up to heaven.

Trance work is like the exchange with nature to which a tree devotes itself. It is nourished by the earth and in turn it nourishes the earth with its vibrations and its beauty— sublime energetic exchange and, at the same time, so simple. The channeler, like the tree, is a vibratory portal between two worlds. The channeler, totally rooted, lets herself be shaken by the wind and by the light that passes through.

Strangely, trance work also resembles a loving exchange where desire is the nourishing sap of the inter-penetration of two hearts. Like the participants in trance, the love partners exchange first of all a non-judgmental loving look. Slowly, one of the two partners becomes more receptive, the other becomes more active. The movement of exchange takes a direction from the active toward the receptive. There is then created an acceptance and a desire to move towards the other person, to penetrate the world of the one who stays receptive, attentive, wanting to hear words of love and able to be seen in complete transparency, to be finally known. In channeling, there is also the extending of oneself towards the other person and the very respectful penetration of that person's world.

The more the person who receives the message accepts, and opens to this penetration, the more the message is deployed with love. The more there is resistance, the more the message shrinks back, and the more the exchange is hindered. The more the exchange flows, the more the channeler is nourished by her work.

The first glance does not take in completely the meaning of what is seen. Everything in nature and in the human is symbolic. Symbols hide, almost completely, the secrets and the sacred of the individual psyche. Ultimate reality lies hidden behind phenomena, signs, and representations. Appearances demonstrate a great power: They shelter what is essential, protecting it from all encroachment. They are the other end, the crude part of subtle energy. They tease the non-initiated eye with a few indicators that are always present and accessible although well hidden. The wearer of appearances, or the client, gains by being paid attention to. In order to discover the meaning behind the image, you need to conduct a shifting of attention from numerous distractions—the appearances—to an inner landscape laid bare where life is played out on a few notes that are measured and full of the essence of the being.

Rational science observes objects; horizontal sexuality observes an object. Vertical sexuality observes the divine. The trance no longer observes anything. The person in trance tends to blend into the other person, allowing herself to be lightly reminded of what is important. Entering into trance is to move from objective consciousness, seemingly objective, to divine consciousness. Christ consciousness is a state of being in which the divine, the unity of all things, and love for the divine are revealed. The trance is a tool for welcoming divine consciousness—or Christ consciousness if that is chosen. It is a tool thanks to which you go about finding unity in each thing by decoding the meaning behind the representation.

Objective Consciousness

Separation, solitude or isolation.
It's a choice. It's a stage to be experienced.

Divine Consciousness

Unity in all things.

Christ Consciousness

Unity in all things according to a vibration of love

Exercises

Breathing: Tasting the Comforting Waves of Prana

To breathe is to be nourished by oxygen and also by the subtle energy of the air, *prana*. One doesn't happen without the other.

While the trance is being induced, a **jerky breathing** (or panting like that of a *little dog*— through the nose or through the mouth) can help deepen the altered state being sought. Taking lengthy, **deep breaths** is also helpful. As is filling your central channel using continuous short breaths that move the air up through the central energetic column. During any channeling, the breathing must remain fluid, easy, without ever being forced. It is good to check its smoothness all during the message. If necessary, you can stop and take a few deep breaths to deepen the state of trance once again if it gets away from you.

Circular breathing practiced for five minutes twice a day supports doing the previous breathings effortlessly during trance work because the energy has been worked on as it is opening. This means breathing consciously, with total presence and leaving out any pause between breathing out and breathing in. The breathing then becomes round. It draws us into a restful rhythm and confirms that we are present to the fullness of our being.

A Meeting with a Guide

Breathe. Relax. Drop all thought, all distraction. Or wrap them into sensations in your body. Let them dissipate in you, around you. Don't keep them running in your head. Right away, set your intention to meet your Guide or a wise and loving person.

Become aware of your third eye. Bring all your attention to this *visionary* space between the eyebrows. You can tap on it lightly with two fingers. Your forehead is alive, perhaps even bubbly. And it is cool.

Turn your subtle eye (or third eye) toward the physical heart. Let this seeing travel to the heart wall and let yourself pass through it. Imagine that your presence is completely full in the physical heart. Then make contact with your subtle energy. Let yourself bathe in a vibration of love.

From this *sacred* heart space, visualize a path in front of you. Set out on this path that winds away in front of you. Where does it lead? What place is revealed? What image appears?

Let this image develop. Like a place of inner meditation— cradling and calming. Visualize the details; ask your imagination for precise details. Let a setting present itself or a beautiful countryside be revealed. Welcome your Guide into this space charged with love and light. Ask Him or Her for the most helpful thing to be said at this moment.

Say that you will come back to this place depending on your needs and ask that you be met there again. Say that you are preparing questions for Him and Her...

Offer thanks...

Part Two

The Art of Life:
Refining Your Inner Vision

*Now you are in your inner space, the place of the Spirit Lake. ...
Each of us has this inner space, but during the lives of most people,
it becomes smaller and smaller. As we go through life, the world
around us tries to fill up and kill this inner space, your Spirit Lake.
Its space is occupied by legions of foreign soldiers, and it dies. ...*

*This next thing is the greatest secret I could ever tell you. We have
the task of building two things while we are in our physical lives.
Our first task is to construct the physical reality in which we live.
The second task is the creation of ourselves—of that very Self that
lives within this outer reality.*

*Both tasks require equal attention. Keeping the balance between
them is a very sacred and demanding art. As soon as we forget one
task, the other can capture us and make us its slave forever. This
is why the place of the Spirit Lake, the home of the Inner Being,
becomes empty and dead for so many people. They come to truly
believe that the outer world is the only one worth their attention.
Sooner or later they will realize their mistake.*

Olga Kharitidi, Entering the Circle

Chapter 9

Evolving

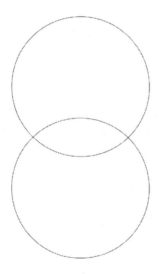

Coming to maturity in your heart means falling in love with the world once again.
Anodea Judith

Like a Tree, From the Roots to the Sky

The oriental science of the chakras asserts as a premise that the evolution of every human being begins from the base and moves upward, from the first chakra or rootedness on up through the upper chakras—sixth, seventh, and eighth—passing through sexuality, action in the world, the heart, and then the soul's expression. This same schema of growth is to be found in the evolution and history of humanity. According to Anodea Judith, author of *Wheels of Life*, we may be on the verge of opening the world's heart chakra. What love for ourselves will we need to develop to fall in love with the world once again as she predicts. What an interesting perspective!

Let's imagine the evolution of this inner world that dwells within us, that calls out to us urgently and that we ought to love boundlessly. Let's close our eyes and be there instantly. Too simple? Not at all. We *are* our inner world and of course we have access to ourselves effortlessly. But do we really want to? Are we ready to inhabit ourselves and be fully present? Do we really want to master this intimate inner seeing that reveals who we are as living beings?

Let's imagine the subjects of our personal domain—their different lives from one personage to another, their age, their communication and their destiny. Let's imagine their growth, from the little child to the wise elder passing by way of the adolescent and the adult in his becoming, one chakra at the time.

First Chakra: The Child

There is a sensitive area in us that shelters and defines our feeling of belonging to humanity. The assurance of being at home on earth, of having a clearly defined place, very much our own place, comes to us from our family, from the emotional connections established from an early age and from the solidity of those connections. The reflection in the body of this feeling can be seen in the gracefulness of our movements and in the ease and beauty of our body whether it is big or little, tall or short, since beauty is a state, not an appearance.

Even though the first chakra corresponds to childhood, it begins its development in the uterus and during the first months of life. This is why it is important to establish a real desire for life in ourselves, especially if our parents did not want us. It is never too late to distill desire for ourselves in the deepest part of our being. And this is why it is equally important to free our body from any limiting thought as we face life.

The psychological health of our present-day inner child, who was developed in our past by the welcoming in and acceptance received from our family of origin, illuminates our relationship to the reality of being united. We belong to a great family, including our personal family and all the communities which constitute humanity. We are not alone. Our actions have an impact on the rest of human life and the actions of humanity influence us and transform our personal lives. We are not only alive but we are alive within an *all* (the totality of everything in and around us) and deeply united to this *all*. Every physical or emotional suffering has its origin in the feeling of separation from this wholeness. We have to live in a responsible way as members of the human tribe, treating ourselves with love as we treat others with love. We have to respect all forms of life on earth, starting with our own bodies.

The term tribe goes beyond the notion of family or group. It connects to an archetype of belonging—the collective identity, the beliefs, the influences and actions of a given group, its strengths and its limitations. The emotional and philosophical inheritance received from our family of origin constitutes the foundation of our identity and consolidates our belonging to a distinct collectivity. We can be in harmony or disharmony with the various elements that make up this inheritance but we must have identified them in order to better define our own makeup. These elements must be the object of continual questioning.

When we recognize our family connections, or our tribal connections, we celebrate our own lives. This is how we deploy our development as an individual in the process of maturing, and in the search for a deep feeling of integration into the whole of humanity.

We can question ourselves on the health of our inner child by evaluating how we are in any group: Do we feel safe in a group? Are we comfortable in our immediate family or in the extended family of such groups as those focused on training, study, personal development or work?

Never forget that we are the only ones to know this personage, this child who persists in our memory. Others are in touch with a young adult or an adult engaged in a process of becoming whole. Let's not impose our childhood suffering on those around us. That suffering concerns only ourselves. We alone have the responsibility and power to heal it.

Second Chakra: The Adolescent

During the adolescence the individual truly begins to desire. Before that, without much awareness, he wanted things that seemed to be able to satisfy his basic needs. Especially his need to be loved unconditionally, to be safe, to be touched, nourished, cared for, socialized and to receive real affection. If these needs were not met or not met sufficiently, he would set about his wanting by imposing *I need* on his *I want*. The less the essential needs were met, the more imperative the *I want* would become.

In childhood, the expression of needs can be shifted to the consumption of toys, sweets, food, for example. In adolescence and later in adulthood, this shift will perhaps be towards the consummation of goods, drugs, alcohol, fast-food or sex. Did our family of origin provide well for the physical and affective survival of the child we used to be? Is there still a *repair job* that needs to be completed? Is there some work waiting to be done with respect to the responsibility, which is now ours, of ensuring that our fundamental needs are met without shifting them onto other people or onto consumables. Wanting is not yet desiring. Wanting is static; desiring is dynamic. True desire doesn't seek to respond to a basic need but is initiated based on already fulfilled needs. It follows then that the sexuality that will arise in the adolescent must be a fully unencumbered sexuality— unencumbered by irrational requirements projected onto the other person.

The adolescent then begins to desire, to set himself in motion, extending his hand towards a second person or a second world. Thanks to a state of stability and a feeling of belonging formed in and by his first family (one hopes!), the individual moves into a state of desire—a reaching out toward another person, the opposite sex, the unfamiliar, *the far away*. How will his ability to desire be expressed? What will be the quality of his desires and how will they be integrated into his personal value system which becomes more defined through distinguishing it from the value system of his first community?

At thirteen, fourteen or fifteen, games of opposition and attraction surface. The individual sets himself up in opposition to authority, to the tribe, to the community, to known ideas, preconceived ideas, to the dependency of childhood. Identity becomes established, the ego develops, sexual identity clarifies, and desire becomes confident. This work on oneself needs to be carried out. The adolescent is attracted by independence, an identity of his own, new ideas, the other sex, or in homosexuality someone with a sexual persona different from his own. Polarity—the duality inherent in all things—appears attractive and becomes a driver for change. The second chakra is where separation takes place whereas the first chakra is the site of union.

Separating from his tribe is at the center of the first real desire of the adolescent. To unite, we have to be able to separate. To separate, we need to have the experience of belonging. To unite, we have to be able to leave the previous union. To really get involved, we have to feel free to leave behind what we were involved in. Being aware of the separation and of the difference and making this awareness one's own creates the desire to unite once again. All of this exists in an infinite and virtuous circle! Has the moving through of each and every stage, belonging or separation, gone well for you? Was it preceded and followed by its opposite?

In order to desire someone else, you have to be identified with yourself. Not indiscriminately with the family, not with your parents. The coming together with the other person contains and fosters the coming together with yourself. Your own identity becomes more clearly defined by doing this. The desire to unite is a lively force that gets us going, sets us in motion and therefore inherently includes the fear of losing and being abandoned by the chosen person—or alternatively of being dominated by that person or by particular life circumstances.

Desire, in its broad meaning, stimulates vitality and creates fluidity and the ability to flow towards *the other*—whether this other is a person, a possession, a creation or a given clientele. The desire for objects is the first stage of maturing during adolescence—objects such as: Money, material possessions, sexual objects, power, appearances. Did adolescence go well for you?

The spiritual work that must finally be conducted is to transform the desire for objects into a desire to meet *the other* embodied in a person with whom one has a loving relationship that is deep and true. Or alternatively to elevate the desired material objects into tools that allow the person to express himself freely as a complete person. This means learning to act in full awareness in our relationships with others. We must manage to create unions (loving, friendly, social or professional) that foster our growth and manage as well to cast off connections that stand in the way of those unions. We must learn to praise others and praise their accomplishments, in spite of their limitations and taking into account their vulnerability as well as their strengths.

The adolescent goes beyond the collective consciousness of the tribe. In considering various childhood situations, he realizes one day that he can make different and effective choices. Later in adolescence he will understand the fundamental reasons underlying the choices that have been made. In doing that, he will be confronted by who he really is. And what better time could there be for a love relationship to facilitate and deepen the work on oneself!

Third Chakra: The Young Adult

The past is the fuel we burn to light our way to the future.
Anodea Judith

Let us move on in our journey through time and the energetic deployment initiated at conception. The image of a form to be expressed in matter is the first movement of the soul towards Earth. Visualizing an image of herself makes the soul a witness to her own existence and supports her manifestation. Incarnating, entering into her human skin, will then take a whole lifetime. Around the age of twenty is specifically the moment when this integration can happen with the greatest effectiveness.

The soul descends to Earth and makes her nest, her cocoon. Around twenty, she finally belongs more firmly to a particular place of existence, a particular location on the electromagnetic grid that envelops the earth. Solitude, mortality, responsibility and embodiment are fundamental elements of information in this inviolable energetic space. I term it inviolable because I am very clear that there cannot be any break or shift in the deep being (except in the case of a homicide). I believe that all wounds to the heart and all wounds to the ego can be healed. Even those that have seemed infinitely destructive.

After having worked to strengthen healthy and sustaining roots (child—first chakra), and then to establish close relationships in which sexuality can begin to open (adolescent—second chakra), next comes the necessity of establishing a supple and evolving interconnection among external work, the pleasures of life, and the inner world with its marvels and its demanding emotions (young adult—solar plexus).

The first three chakras form a physical and temporal trilogy. Through exploring these very human territories, the person seeks to rise more and more toward a subtle, sacred state that will lead her or him to the divine.

At the time of moving from the adolescent to the young adult, the soul begins to look at its environment with a more and more human perspective. The astral moves away; life calls. This call is incarnated in others, groups or individuals, drawing the soul into the human net. The healthy ego continues to develop. Accent is put on the external, on separation, and on the illusory un-union with others and with life. The result is an separation with his own center—we could go so far as to say with his own soul. The young adult seeks to preserve this un-union. He cultivates it, in fact, he has to cultivate it. In defining himself he is less in opposition than he was in adolescence, but he continues to count on the difference without yet recognizing the similarity. He is perfecting the construction of his ego and his identity.

He gets involved in new social, professional and relational milieus. The quest to find himself is ongoing thanks to his social and professional involvement. The search for balance is never more active and fascinating than that of the young adult. Perhaps you are still a young adult in certain aspects of your personality. In my case, I completed (or almost completed—nothing being ever totally complete) this obligatory stage only a few years ago when receiving my master's degree. The different stages of maturing do not follow one after each other. They intersect, mix together or overlay each other, and they do not necessarily follow each other in chronological order. At any time, one of them can be picked up, reworked and finalized. All unrealized potential remains and awaits only our agreement in order to manifest and complete an earlier stage that was skipped.

Through work at the level of the solar plexus, the individual, in response to the process of individuation that he attempts to enter into, seeks to become open to modes of consciousness that are situated beyond the simply rational—intuition for example, and also gut instincts. He begins to understand that individual power, which is impossible to divide up, is really expressed in the material world and that he manifests his life on the material plane from his inner sun. He conducts inner-business. He invests variously in his emotions. The moral dividends begin to be significant.

The child seeks to become part of the collective consciousness based on healthy relationships with his family of origin. The adolescent establishes a link with someone close on whom he projects his own image so he can recognize himself. He portends the lover that is inner or made inner and the emotional health of his own future family.

The young adult is more conscious of himself. He understands more about who he is and he is ready to move deeper into self-knowledge. To do this he expands his activities—those that are social and especially those that are professional. He becomes more creative in doing this. He becomes aware of his power. He therefore has a chance of grasping its profound nature and of using this power advisedly in the material world. He manages to define himself better as his own person—an essential condition for his personal accomplishment in the world. As if he had been standing firmly but motionless, and then, realizing that movement was possible, he finally gets going. Going where he needs to go—straight ahead.

And so, moving from childhood to adolescence and on to adulthood, an important threshold is crossed in the twenties. Was it really in the twenties for you? At one moment or another, we all undergo an experience that will contribute to revealing the strengths and weaknesses that are part of our individual nature and which exist outside the influence of our elders: A first pregnancy, a heartbreak, a serious illness, the loss of a job. Such experiences can be initiatory. Subscribing to self-awareness is part of an experience of initiation or of a rite of passage. It is beginning to find your life's direction. Without that you will encounter emptiness. We must accept the responsibility of living according to the characteristics that define us and, since in our culture there are no organized rites of passage, we must grasp the meaning of ordeals or important events imposed by life and use them as a bridge to pass from one stage to another. That can happen in one leap or one little step at a time. In primitive societies, an organized initiation rite would allow the tribe to recognize what the individual has become. In the West, this recognition is often missing because there are no longer initiation rites or they are flawed. Therefore, we need to deeply accept ourselves.

The history of what we have lived through—in this life and in past lives—emerges and can circulate freely through our earthly being and through the initial workings of our life. Our life presages what our future experiences will be.

Our first successes—social, amorous or professional— develop our self-esteem or the feeling of being worth one's weight in gold.

Self-esteem is reflected in our lives just as surely and precisely as in a mirror. Our accomplishments lead us to declare respect for ourselves, to recognize ourselves and to bless ourselves. This is the principal lesson of this stage of life.

Fourth Chakra: The Adult

> *However, I have not lived until now in vain: Love—that keenness mixed with courage, violence and caring which has meant that humanity has adopted its name for all time—I have come to know it well. It has been my highest task—and also the most disturbing.*
> Jean-François Beauchemin

The experience of love takes place through all the passing years. Our life transforms our ability to love and love transforms our life. Through many a holding back, regrouping and reopening we are allowed access to more balance and maturity.

After loving our immediate family—most often unconditionally—we open to a circle of external individuals not connected to us by blood. We enlarge our tribe. Then we begin to affirm ourselves in the professional and social worlds. We *love* objects that we acquire, we work, we travel, and we build an identity that is both fuller and more personal than our initial tribal identity. We are young adults. **And our domain is the whole Earth and its materiality.** Our physical world is well established and supports our development. In any case, this is a reality that we must move towards.

However, **our domain must become one of the heart and of its intangibility.** We are opening to an inner life that is richer and to a more fulfilling love of ourselves—and therefore of others. Thanks to our successful journeying, which is never done, through the ego and through matter, we reach the intangible. We reach a more authentic and nourishing love. Slowly, a certain maturity begins to live in us. We owe it to ourselves to become emotionally stable. That doesn't mean no longer experiencing emotion or no longer expressing emotion. We are brought back to face the responsibility of healing our hearts and of not entering into relationships with others based on old wounds but instead in full awareness and with compassion.

Thanks to the love that we develop for ourselves, it becomes possible to marry opposites in ourselves—a symbolic marriage of all parts of who we are. Our human life is united with the soul or our divine life. This marriage is represented by the cross: the verticality of our life joined at its very center with the already established horizontal. And quite rightly, it is just about at that exact moment that the first legal marriages take place!

In channeling, we pledge to respect our own needs on the affective plane in order to better care for those consulting us. In so doing, we succeed in accepting our clients unconditionally without bringing in an emotional charge that belongs only to us. This is facilitated by the professional state that we enter into with clients. On the other hand, we must constantly question what is taking place in our heart in other spheres of our social and private life.

During our adolescence, we separated from our parents at first. That allowed us to establish our search for the foundations of our independence. Then, as young adults we set ourselves up professionally with a certain degree of success. In any case, we now earn our livelihood and we live our lives. We continue to acquire more maturity in our relationships and in our work by developing our strength, our sense of compassion, and our communication skills, by deepening our knowledge and by enlarging our competence. Toward the middle of our lives (at the time of our mid-life crisis or was it a little before or a little after your forties?), it is possible that events or serious illness might have overturned the confidence we had of being in control of our lives and of being able to create what we wanted.

Thanks to certain difficult moments (divorce, losing a job, ending a relationship, illness, burnout) we are forced to take stock of our personal limits and realize that we are unable (or not as able as we thought) to fulfill our desires. The plans we made and the objectives we pursued are sometimes rendered null and void. Can we continue to love life under such circumstances? Critical events lead us to ask ourselves deep questions. What is the meaning of my life? Do I manage to stimulate positive change in the destiny of the world—am I doing my part in that? Am I part of a universal project that is more vast and morally more elevated than my personal projects? Do I intend to adapt myself to the changes? Do I need help? Do I treat myself with as much respect as I treat others or my clients? Discovering what we can give to others is to discover what we can give to ourselves; it is discovering how to love.

There is no possible healing for the body without a healing of the heart. Harboring grudges or feelings of vengeance—and it's the same with guilt—is toxic for the body. Lack of forgiveness when one has hard feelings towards oneself or others is a poison for the soul as well as for the body and it weakens affective and energetic resources. However, the road leading to forgiveness must be travelled slowly—with attention, care and discernment. Otherwise the ordeals we undergo will not offer up all their riches. Forgiveness opens the heart chakra as long as it is not pursued too hastily.

Fifth Chakra: the Mature Adult

At this particular moment... the divine prevails over the
physical being.
Joseph Campbell

At one moment or another, in one way or another, we have
been faced with fundamental choices. We had to realize that
we are never alone and yet we have lived as if nothing or no one
could bring us real support. Learning to communicate our deep
questioning in order to begin to find essential answers to the
development of our way of being in the world is a significant
lesson attached to this stage of life.

Causality—the search for causes of our misfortunes and of
the accusations leveled against certain protagonists in our
story—must give way to intentionality. What has amounted
to a carelessness in the past must now give way to the ability
to adopt a firm intention so we can, in the present moment,
work on ourselves with clarity without any accusations leveled
against oneself, others, life or even the divine.

This is the time when involvement in constructing a healthy
connection with the material world must be balanced by an
equal involvement with higher moral values. We need to
exercise our will to achieve the accomplishment of our new
objectives. And we need to articulate them clearly in ourselves
in order to carry their expression to the outer world.

Up to now our choices have been more or less responsible, more
or less lucid. We have exercised our responsibility. Now there
is a movement to mature our will. The choices are clearer, self-
mastery is greater and the accomplishment of our desires takes

place more naturally. Our self-expression and our life mission as well as the communication of our emotions become more refined, more mature, and more creative.

Maturity demands that once again we put ourselves into question. We have to adopt a new vision with respect to the nature of our individual power—a power that gradually gives way to divine will.

The Upper Chakras: the Sage

How do you define spirituality? Divinity? Your mediumistic talent? What does the spirit world represent for you? Where are you at in your spiritual development? Are your moral values clearly identified and do they support your actions?

Introspection, that slow, constant and methodical work of self-evaluation, of self-knowledge, has done its work in our inner *fort*. It stimulates the involvement of emotional intelligence. Connections are woven among our emotions, our personality and our moral sense. We refine our ability to analyze our attitudes and our behavior. That allows us to profit from our experiences, enlarge and enrich our lives and deepen our knowledge of ourselves.

Giving value to the inner life, giving it its place in day-to-day life and in the work of channeling is important because, whether we like it or not, it exists and keeping it in the dark is to deny a whole aspect of ourselves.

In this way wisdom begins to flourish in our inner world. We discern life's lessons, which our experiences provide for us and we attain detachment—the ability to let go while still remaining open as we set aside the associative mind so we can be more present to our bodies and to the whole of our being.

Caroline Myss in *Anatomy of the Spirit* gives us an example: "Take for instance, the truth 'Change is constant.' Mentally we can absorb that teaching with little difficulty. Yet when change occurs in our lives ... this truth terrorizes us. We often need years to recover from some changes because we had hoped that it—whatever 'it' was—would remain the same. We knew all along that it would change, but we can't help hoping that the energy of change will pass by this one part of our lives."

Adopting a detached attitude when facing change bolsters our confidence in a helpful turn-around. It is difficult to not resist change. On the other hand, giving oneself to the present moment and to all the unexpectedness and instability that it contains allows us to feel more unified and less in conflict with life and the order of things. We get energy from that.

Wisdom, developed from recognizing and embracing a spiritual life, calms us. This allows us to open ourselves to others and to develop the altruism necessary for work with a given clientele or in the service of humanity. Consciousness moves towards a quest for the divine or toward higher moral values and a sense of human dignity.

The chakras allow energy to pass from low to high, and forward. They activate the energy little by little. The heart reaches its maturity, and thanks to the deployment of our inner life, the world in all of its grandeur is loved... infinitely!

Chapter 10

Grounding

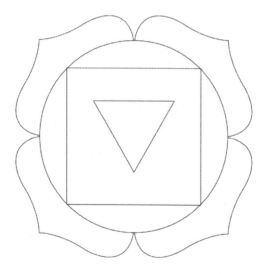

It is a pity not to be able to remember the first time we learned how to walk: The day when the world—instead of being reduced to the swaying of the cradle, to the smoothness of a ceiling, to the leaves of a tree—rose up before us and, offering itself for our independent journeying, showed itself to be inexhaustible.
Chantal Thomas

Grounding?

To be grounded: What a curious expression!
Am I a tree, a plant, a flower?

Why are my feet so far away from my head? Why does my mind try so hard to distance me from my body where my consciousness resides? Why do we say of someone that he's flying high or that he doesn't have both feet on the ground? Or that he's *off the wall*? Do we think he'll fly away like a bird?

My roots are invisible and yet they're very real. Looking at my body and the deployment of its aura, its subtle energy, I discover that I am immense. My body extends in all directions. My arms embrace the whole Earth, my hair entangles with the clouds and carries me up to the sky. My heart remembers still those loved ones who passed long ago and it already has love for the humanity to come. All distortions due to linear time and all distances are transcended by the vastness of my being. I am far beyond space and time, present to everything, all at the same time. So, why could not my roots burrow down to the center of the earth, contact its fire and receive its energy?

When my eyes close, I am instantly in my inner world—there is no exile, no fleeing, no wandering lost. I look and see myself, wandering sometimes it is true, but nevertheless a tender voyageur in a domain peopled by every living element on Earth. Because I was born and I was raised in a village, nature is an archetype that developed in my inner world. My native village has enlarged and has become the entire universe. Numerous landscapes inhabit me. Trees assemble in luxuriant forests, brooks becomes creeks, creeks become streams, and streams become rivers and oceans. The hill in front of my parent's house is the

Everest that I heroically conquered. Why would I be less than all that is living? I am the queen of my kingdom and of all of my subjects. I am I, I am the others, I am the Earth. The first chakra, the chakra of rootedness, refers to the unity of the world...

In the expanse of my intimate panoramas, my ancestors beat a path among the obstacles created by my absences from my history. They accept to stand in the very middle of my life without needing all my attention. They watch out for the tribe that brought me into the world. My childhood toys and books are resting in an airy attic room. My memories are piled up there in diligently labeled boxes. My childhood is safeguarded and cared for. All those people with whom I have come in contact in the course of the years remain present in me. These living elements, although they are in the background, underlie my existence and give it a substantial and vibrating consistency. My life bears fruit.

My body and its subtle extension contain all of me and carry my life of yesterday, today and tomorrow. My distant past, my present and my future are inscribed in my cells without determinism but with conviction. I am living from long ago and for always and I know it. I am rooted in my human life just as completely as in the life of my soul.

For a long time, I believed I had to root myself more and more by extending my roots toward or into the earth. I have walked a lot in my life, sometimes consciously, sometimes very distractedly. Ungrounding myself, going into my head, turning my attention away from nature are practices that I'm good at. I walked with more or less consciousness until the day when I understood that, if I kept myself in a receptive state, it would be the earth that would do all the work. It is the Earth that will nourish me to the small extent that I welcome her in. It is not up to me to try to do so much. With time, I allowed myself to be penetrated by the certainty and by the really helpful sensation of being nourished, supported, protected by the earth and by all that she brings of beauty, living beings and love.

Caring for One's Past

If you no longer know where you're going, look at where you've come from.
African proverb

What about your past? What remains in your body from your first tribe?

The children that we have been were born as part of a certain tribe in a specific geographic location and in a certain era. This tribe increased with time—it evolved in us, for us, and by us. Today we are the result of the totality of those elements transmuted by the love offered to and received from each person we have met in all the places and in all the moments since our birth. Sometimes, it was the lack of love that shaped us. There's no escaping this...

In the course of the unfolding of our personal growth, we need to try to preserve positive tribal imprints and to turn away from those that harm us or harm others. The basic beliefs of a tribe are strong and tend to lead each individual to conform to a certain conglomerate image. This tendency is very strong in Western society. We could mention for example the image of a certain feminine body based on appearance and not on being. Certain beliefs no longer suit us, others acquire more weight.

Our physical bodies, our minds and our hearts are really energized by new ideas or by old ideas in dynamic evolution.

We owe it to ourselves to also enlarge our personal history, to deepen our understanding of it by placing it in the context of the history of the world. It takes a load off our backs. We no longer feel alone.

Bringing care to childhood wounds and healing one's past improves our relationships with members of our original tribe and, by extension, with the human tribe.

Think of your childhood... What expression or expressions describe it best? Positive or negative? What remains of that in your adult life? What is the next stage of integration or of healing in relation to your childhood? The redemption of your childhood could be accomplished by writing or recounting once again certain of its most important or painful moments. An intention to heal must however be paramount in your retelling of it in order to enjoy the greatest liberation.

Do you know your parents well? For example, what are their exact dates of birth? This is a question I often ask and you would be amazed, as I am, to realize that people don't know their parent's exact age!

Do you really know your parents? The emotional landscape of their birth? Their happiness and their pain? Their wars and their victories? The same questions apply for your grandparents, for your brothers and sisters and even for your ancestors. How can you go forward without knowing where you've come from?

What remains in your heart of their beliefs, of their values, of their limits and of their heroism? Where in your body do you find strands of your own history, as well as the history of your parents and your ancestors?

What are your needs in relation to your family, to humanity in general and to any group in particular?

How do you differentiate your needs? Do you respond to your needs and the needs of others most of the time? Do you respond to the deep need of your being or to the need to attract attention or provoke someone? Is your attention directed outward or toward the center of yourself?

> *It's never to late to have a happy childhood.*
> Tom Robbins

Gratitude Meditation

> *"Bring your awareness to your base energy center. This spot is charged with love and will allow you to reconnect with the mother-aspect that desires you. Because even if you did not deeply feel the desire of your physical mother for you, your spiritual mother, in contrast, from her goodness, wanted you to be on Earth. This desire, coming from Mother-Earth, to give you life— you have to find it again and make it your own."*
> Message from Guides

Take a few deep breaths. Let go...

Breathe quietly, naturally. The back is held quite straight, effortlessly, in full relaxation. Be totally present to yourself in a state of great receptivity...

Give thanks to your ancestors, to your great human family which has brought you to this point and which will carry you further within time. Give thanks for the living inheritance that you have received up to now, and for the environment that sustains you in spite of all the abuse that it has received. Commit yourself to leaving a habitat for your children that is healthier, more nourishing and more beautiful than the one that has sheltered your life. Don't weigh yourself down with the loss of what has been, of what could have been, but imagine the possibility of repairing what remains, and of vivifying what is. Give thanks for the beauty of the world!

Express your gratitude for the circle of all those with whom you engage professionally, socially, intimately. They are accepting to create a new tribe, a new place of love for the healing of initial wounds. Commit to nourishing humanity with your presence and your knowledge.

Thank Mother Earth who carries you with such generosity although she is suffering. Thank all the Light Beings who are present with you on your life path. Your Guides are part of your spiritual tribe. Feel their presence day by day.

Give thanks, give thanks...

Caring for your Body

Mastery of the first chakra consists essentially in understanding and healing the body. Learn to accept your body, to feel it, to validate it, and to love it. These are the challenges that await us.
Anodea Judith

The reality of the body is an exact image of the essential nature of the being. The strength of the soul resides in the body. If the body is denied, a great part of the richness of the life is lost. The conscious taking of responsibility for the life—in all its dimensions, in all of its fullness—takes place in the body. The head is only a relay station.

What am I doing these days for my body, to care for it? Have I had a massage lately? Have I received any bodywork in the last year? How is my eating regime? Do my life routines look out for my body and for me in the best way possible? Do they support my desire to live and to serve humanity? Do I love myself physically? Be careful. It's not a matter of saying that you will love yourself when you get to the right weight or when your face starts to look younger. No, it means to really love your body—as you are now. Do you know your body well? Could you look at yourself in a mirror for a stretch of some minutes with no judgment?

Our whole existence is written in our body. By visiting it from inside we learn what it has to say and we discover all parts of our deep being in doing that.

The following meditative visualization is to be repeated, at your own pace, the whole of it or just small parts of it, according to your needs. Slowly, awareness of the body becomes like a way of living day-to-day. The body is no longer ever left behind, ignored or put to sleep. It is always vibrating with a beautiful and comforting presence. Pain and discomfort happen rarely...

Many people are already fully present to their bodies. They may then wonder how to take it further, more deeply—through a warm feeling toward a body that is a friend, not an enemy. This visualization fosters the development of the relationship with the body. Since the body is related to the first chakra, all bodywork harmonizes this chakra.

Visualization for Grounding

Settling yourself comfortably or walking slowly outside, take a few deep breaths. And bring your full awareness to your body.

First of all bring your attention to the root chakra, between the anus and the genitals. At the very tip of the coccyx, between the vulva and the anus or between the testicles and the anus, is lodged the root of the being, coiled upon itself, and very alive. Feel this spot. Imagine this point of energy lengthening, extending down, up and in all directions, like a sun that radiates and illuminates your relationship with Mother Earth, with life, with humanity.

Feel its vibration and breathe through it, contracting a little the muscles around it—a very gentle contraction, then let go. Contraction... letting go—a few times. In this way you will manage to lead your awareness into this point which is the physical relay station of the root chakra. (You can locate this point using a mirror or feeling it with your fingers. Is the muscle tone good? Or is it sagging? Good tone means good grounding; sagging lets you know the grounding is inadequate. In sexual relations, when it is massaged gently orgasmic energy is awakened, relaxation moves through and the doorway upward opens.)

Maintain this contact between your awareness and the first chakra, and set out on a tour of your body. The breathing is gentle and regular. You are aware without your attention to the breathing distracting you from the exploration of the physical aspect of the first chakra.

How are your legs today? Are they tired? Light? Are they more or less present? Have you thought of your feet today? Your toes, your ankles? Is there a discomfort or a lack of energy in your lower body? In your feet, in your legs, your calves, your thighs? Are you paying attention to your legs? Today only? Almost never? Often? Always? Do you have the impression that your legs are well integrated into the rest of your body? Breathe into them... breathe for them...

Now bring your attention to your pelvis. Making a few contractions of the pelvic muscles you can feel the root chakra with more precision. The contractions/releases bring more blood into this area. A bit of heat gets created. You can also feel the whole of the energy there in your pelvis. Is there a certain heat? Or is it more like an emptiness? More tense or more relaxed? Do you have the impression that your body is positioned on your pelvis, on the buttock bones, on the buttocks? Are you seated on a foundation, on something solid or is something missing? Simply by thinking of it, by bringing your attention and intention to it, the pelvic energy awakens and the heat spreads out more completely. The blood pours into your pelvis, into pelvic muscles, into your genital organs. Accept this life which is yours, which vibrates within you.

Bring your attention a little higher up in the belly and you will be able to feel your kidneys, perhaps. Imagine: Your kidneys are like two little embryo-shaped seeds. Above them, above the kidneys are the adrenals—little capsules that are pyramidal in shape. Try to feel your kidneys and the adrenal glands. You can get there more easily from the back. You can even place your hands at the level of the kidneys—it's fairly high up—just below the diaphragm. When you enter into contact with your kidneys, what do they say? Do they speak to you about their fatigue? Do they tell you about their vitality? Are they happy? Or are they really afraid? When you bring your awareness into the kidneys, does your mouth become a little dry? Or, on the contrary, wetter? The kidneys are not stuck on the skin of the back. When we talk about the kidney area on the back, we usually mean the small of the back. However, the kidneys are right in the middle of the body. They form a bridge between the upper and lower body. Between the front and the back of the body also. You can make contact with them just as well from the front as from the back. They are really a mid-point, a rallying point for everything. They participate in the foundation of your being, of your personality, of your energy. Thank them for their work.

Around your kidneys you will feel your digestive system. Imagine its action of kneading and assimilation. Feel how you are hugely nourished in all the fibers of your being by the food you ingested earlier.

Now move up a little higher in your body. Is your breathing smooth enough? If it seems right, respond to the need to take big deep breaths. Is your heart calm? Is it open? Is it present? Do your lungs open easily?

Bring your awareness into your shoulders, into your arms, your elbows, your forearms, your wrists, your hands, your fingers. Relax them. Do you sense obstacles? Does a pain make itself known? Breathe into spots that seems less warm, less inhabited or more painful. Breathe into those places where your body speaks of its needs. Enter your throat. Is your head positioned in such a way that your throat is open and fully visible? Raise the head a little to give your throat more room. Try to bring your head just a bit back if it was to far forward, but not if it was already straight. And then, bring your attention to your face and relax it. Be aware of your skin, of your cheeks, of your eyelids which are very heavy on your eyes. The forehead can relax, must relax. The forehead is cool. The mouth can be open a little. The jaw can relax, must relax.

Your body is here. It offers itself to you. It is woken up by what you have just done. Have a feeling of recognition and gratitude for your body which serves you for all of your days, which brings you into relationship with others, which makes you alive, which allows you to experience what you experience, to do the work that you do, which allows you to make love, to embrace people and children, to see the beauty of nature, to hear music.

Honor this body that serves you and tell it that, if there are places where you abuse it, if there is a little abuse in your relationship with your body, you are deciding today that the abuse has ended, or that it is beginning to end.

There you are. You have done the rounds of your physical body. Bring your awareness now more precisely to the level of your muscles. Are there places in your body that are more tense, that show you the need for your attention, for your caring? Feel the subtle energy, the subtle messages which are stored in your muscles and therefore in your posture. Who are you in relation to this beautiful substance that you inhabit? Try to feel the deep reaches of your chest, the totality of your heart, of your lungs, of your diaphragm. May be, by thinking of that and in penetrating this vibratory part of your being, you are already a little more in your associative mind. You had a distraction or two—you were thinking of something else. It's a little as if you were carrying your thoughts in your body and around your heart. Go now to your heart, into the depths of your heart. Be aware that you are a divine being. You are a being made of matter, a human with his limits and his beauty. You are also a being who is absolutely divine, absolutely beautiful, absolutely valuable, absolutely marvelous. You have existed for a long time and you will be around for numerous lifetimes still. Give thanks for this moment, this little 80 to 100 years that you have to live in this very beautiful body which is yours. Let yourself expand upward, to the right, to the left, forward, backward and down. Integrate all parts of yourself in a huge feeling of love for everything that you are including all that you would like to be no longer.

Take a few big breaths and gently come back to where you are without leaving this full contact that you have had with your body and with all its vibratory gradations.

Give thanks...

> "To quiet the mind is to spread peace little by little through the channel of the heart. This quietness is connected to fullness in the body. It won't be the intellect that is going to offer you a way out. Nourish yourself by what you feel deeply in your body. Don't hurry. Take your time."
> Message from Guides

Present to Oneself

The first chakra evokes our union with all that is. It gives the feeling that the place occupied energetically on Earth in our first tribe, in the families and groupings where we subsequently worked, is legitimate and even intended. Has this place for you been claimed? Known? Honored? Do you know how it is constructed?

The root chakra is the foundation of our physical and psychological being. Its energy illuminates the markers we received in childhood and gives a general orientation to our personal and professional life. It also structures our learning related to the material world, allowing us to draw numerous teachings from it.

When this chakra is in a state of need, we feel isolated even when in a group. We no longer know how to recognize the splendor of life and of Mother Earth. On the contrary, we abuse our body and destroy our environment. We turn our attention to the accumulation of material goods which never satisfy us, even when in abundance. We feel as though we're drifting, with no definite aim and with no will. We are not acquainted with the body and we abuse it with excessive consummation of all kinds (alcohol, unhealthy food, overeating, hyper-sexuality, etc.).

When this chakra is open, connections built with our human tribe sustain us and delight us. These connections are to be found in our contact with our Mother Earth, in the act of celebrating her and respecting her. We are proud to be who we are and to be human. We demonstrate a good sense of justice, of integrity and of devotion because fear no longer controls every one of our actions. We develop a feeling of belonging which makes us feel safe. Above all, we are in a position to receive *nourishment* directly from Mother-Earth.

Our awareness of the body is developed in such a way as to lead us, within the unfolding of daily life, to feel deeply the needs of our body and to respond to these needs with discernment and fairness.

In trance work: Some wrong ideas are unfortunately too widespread among light workers. The most harmful is the belief that we have to sacrifice our human life for the benefit of our spiritual life— that the two are separate which is a relic of our Judeo-Christian education. However, the placement of the first chakra in the physical body instructs us in the fact that spiritual development begins with a descent into matter and then continues upward by integrating each aspect of our lives.

An open first chakra facilitates a great presence to oneself. The best tool for arriving at this opening is in our walking as we consciously extend ourselves down into the earth. And during that extending the earth extends into us, nourishing our energy, and augmenting our basic vitality. This work of receiving telluric food is too often missing in spiritual work...

For Better Grounding

Walking: the ideal exercise for fostering harmony in the first chakra

Walking Towards Unity

Walking opens and dilates the base chakra, the grounding chakra. The image of the serpent that bites his tail describes very well this energy center situated at the base of the spinal column. We find the serpent in iconic oriental representations and in the image of the Virgin Mary standing on what the Catholic Church considers to be a reality to be destroyed. The serpent turns back towards himself, doubles back on himself—like time, like life. You could say that he stuck his foot in his mouth or that he's got his shoes on the wrong feet! He's in survival mode, self-preservation mode—defending himself from and against everything—like the dragon, that serpent of fire, described by Joseph Campbell in *Transformations of Myth through Time*. He cannot use his life—all he can do is guard it, Campbell tells us, for as long as he has not been able to bring about a leap of freedom, a vertical movement, he remains in reaction, clinging to life, desperately stuck in the world of illusion. The first chakra is an energy wheel of survival. Everything begins there. The energetic base is a socket that must ensure the solidity of the whole physical and subtle edifice. The descent toward this foundation and its conscious integration preparing for a movement upward are necessary for personal development, spiritual awakening and the development of mediumistic talent.

Walking in nature whips up the vital energy represented by a *sleeping* serpent and obliges it to strike out toward what is higher, toward the future in a beautiful creative burst that will lead it to the end of the cultural and social limits established in the past.

In *La marche, un mouvement vital (Walking: a Movement of Life)*, Christina Cuomo shows how walking gives birth to the psychology of the human being and she also shows the extent to which walking modulates the evolution of our immune system. She adds that through this *breaking in of the body* or this apprenticeship through walking, each person "develops their proprioception, builds their posture and outlines in their head a map of the body or a body schema. From the neurological point of view, walking stimulates the functional integrity of all the response systems of the organism. From a psychological point of view: The archetypical movements—keys to the construction of the neurological endocrine-immune network and of life in the vertical—are an excellent means for access to self-recognition, stimulating immunity and reshaping one's silhouette, the perimeter of the body."

Walking is a symbol of spiritual advancement. It allows for a better rootedness in the human world, promotes emotional flow, initiates a descent to ensure a movement upward and prepares for an increased vibration level. The basic movements of the body during walking stimulate life channels such as the meridians but also the subtle channels, the *nadis*. Therefore, at the same time that the joints, muscles and viscera respond to this stirring up of the energy that Cuomo is speaking of, all the subtle bodies are touched, stirred, transformed and vitalized.

Walking was a driving force in my spiritual development. It set markers along my soul's evolutionary path. It called me back to the presence of my body and its language. Once again body awareness was at the center of my movement forward.

What is your own movement in the direction of full development of your being, of your life? Physically, how do you set off toward yourself. In India, yoga has long been a concrete marker in the work towards enlightenment. For others, dance—the art of inhabiting one's body with awareness—is also a spiritual manifestation. For others, sport represents the best way of balancing their lives. There is not just one way of finding your body, inhabiting it and consecrating it. There are many ways. What is yours?

Exploration Exercise in Walking— Outside or in a Big Space

First of all walk the way you usually do without paying attention to your movement or your direction. For a few minutes. Stop and take mental note of the inner state that this exercise has taken you to.

Then walk with awareness. For several minutes. All your attention is in your feet, your legs, then in the movements of your body and in the direction that you give to your walking. Observe the swinging of your arms, the suppleness of your pelvis or its rigidity, the tension or relaxation in your shoulders, the position of your head. Stop and take mental note of the feeling in your body.

Walk with your head down, taking note of your emotional state. Then, walk with the head up but not lifting up the chin, the throat open and the horizon appears. Imagine that a helium balloon is rising in your head and pulling you up without muscular force. How do you feel?

Continue your walk looking at the floor or the ground, then directing your gaze out into the distance. Walk quickly. Slowly. Then backwards. Compare the effects of these various ways of walking on your inner state.

Walk slowly with your eyes open, then with your eyes closed.

Come back to standing still: Imagine a column of red energy, red light, which enters through the top of the head and travels through all the chakras right down into the earth. You need to align your chakras one after the other for the energy to pass. Now make the opposite movement, letting the energy move up. As it moves through, it activates all of your body and each of the chakras.

In the Course of Your Daily Life

Ground Yourself... and Smile!

Practice sports or games of grounding— those that activate the blood circulation in the legs and keep the feet warm. Contemplate nature. Walk barefoot on the grass, on the sand of the seashore. Hug a tree, put your back up against its trunk, lounge around under its shade, listen to it.

Re-create ties with Mother Earth— by gardening for example, or perhaps with repeated sojourns in the country. Make good use of city parks.

When I started walking again systematically, a wonderful little exercise allowed me to gain maximum benefit from my walks: smiling. At first, I had to force myself to smile— not at anyone or about anything— it wasn't easy. The trying gives smiles a bit of a saddened air. Then I decided to smile more at the people I met because I needed an external support. I noticed surprise on a lot of the faces. Sometimes however I received a frank and direct response, a recognition. People are so alone that they manage sometimes to appreciate contact, even with strangers. Then I started to smile at trees, at nature, at life with gratitude, even on gloomy days. Smiling even when confronted by the busying of city folk, faced with their hurry, their not being there. Finally, I was able to smile in the void, without an object, without a thought. Gently, happiness began to be part of my life more consistently.

Chapter 11

Reuniting

Like my body, my sexuality is sacred and I have the full right to enjoy them both. Meeting another person through my sexuality has been an instrument for meeting with myself and with my divinity. Purely and simply.
Passage from my diary

Reuniting

The mystery of sexuality is made up of a thousand facets each one more amazing than the last. More than any other concept, it's the dualistic nature of sexuality that is not understood. The individual tries to live it all of a piece, just one way—today like yesterday, or like tomorrow, or like others do, following well established criteria (for example, orgasm at any price) and following reductionist, imprisoning stereotypes. However...

... sexual energy is not static. It contracts and expands; it's expressed in a feminine way or in a masculine way in men and in women. Vibrations of the sexual partners are raised or lowered. Sexual energy moves up to the brain and down to the feet all at the same time, almost simultaneously, in an infinite dance. It can be experienced with little presence, in solitude, or in a relationship—or with passion in those moments out of time. Nothing is totally negative or totally positive. All the opposites complete each other and support each other, interpenetrate each other. One becomes the other becomes the one becomes the other... The movements of sexuality, the nuances of sexuality, its various ages—each one more interesting than the next—are misunderstood or even rejected. Desire, the most capricious, floating, uncertain thing in loving relationships, is the ultimate symptom of the great versatility of sexuality. It's like always-moving water that flows away as soon as you want to take it in hand.

The concepts of masculine and feminine do not refer to the stereotypes recognized by a society that focuses on the division between them. They are not negative. The masculine is present in everything that is feminine. The feminine is present in everything that is masculine. Sexuality is the harmonious dance—or so often unharmonious dance—between masculine and feminine, between the sacred and the profane. There is a time for the sacred and a time for the profane, but how do we connect the two in a unifying awareness? For example: Make every day a Sunday that is different and the same? Be in one's Sunday best during the dull drag of weekdays? Wear pajamas, a negligee or nudity with elegance and sensuality every day?

Do you have the inner freedom to follow a number of paths in your sexual life each one quite different from the others and all of them elevating? Do you know how to integrate feminine energy and masculine energy in yourself ?

I am offering here a few elements of reflection on sexuality. Organizing them into various types of sexuality—profane, intimate and sacred—is completely personal. This dividing up of reality allows me to present a few ideas in a coherent fashion. I'm making this division to help in understanding; but sexuality is global, immediate and *reuniting*...

Depending on the author and the tradition, the second chakra does not always correspond to sexuality. Sometimes, sexuality is situated in the first chakra. Sometimes, the second is the chakra of the spleen, of creativity and the expression of emotions. Certainly, the pelvic area is connected to the initial life force, to life impulses, to sexual and sacred energy—which is why the word *sacred* is given to some vertebrae.

Isn't it fascinating that the chakra which opens to the sacred, which initiates and facilitates it, is to be found right in the body? New Age beliefs situate the sacred in the upper chakras, almost outside the body, whereas the wisdom traditions situate the sacred at the base of the body—in fact, at the beginning of life. Life energy finds its niche in the pelvis and begins to rise up from the lower body. Its moving up is spiritual because it is trying to connect with the energy of the spirit.

Sacred is connected to the word secret, from the Latin *secernere*, set aside, or *secare* which means separate. *Secare* would have also given birth to the word sex. If the first chakra, the chakra of rootedness, refers to total union with the earth, the tribe, the family, groups, and humans, the second brings us up against a first division, a duality, a difference that tries to reunite in order to create life, to flow towards the other in order to return to the initial union.

> *It is here (in the sacred chakra) that our initial unity becomes duality. Our point becomes a line and gives it a direction which divides unity in two. We circulate then from the element earth to the element water—at the place where solid becomes liquid, where immobility becomes movement, where form becomes formless. In that, we have gained a certain degree of freedom, but also of complexity.*
> Anodea Judith

Horizontal or Profane Sexuality: Passionate Love

The First Journey Toward Oneself

Passionate love is a love of suffering, a violent, impetuous movement towards the other being, or more precisely toward the object of one's desire. It does not brook any constraints but it meets so many of them. It is a necessary and desirable stage that supports the learning of raw pleasure that grounds you. However, with the passage of time, it demands to be refined.

Sexuality is not just something happening in the genitals. That is on the path but it is not limited to that one energetic location. The search to let go of sexual tension represses orgasmic energy and calmly (or rapidly!) turns off real desire.

On its darker side, passionate love counts on genital pleasure, the letting go of tensions and the objectified feminine body. In its more enlightened aspect it begins to illuminate the center of oneself and it can be initiatory.

What is profane is not to be rejected or condemned. Instead it needs to find its rightful place and be used so we can evolve. Profane means *facing the door*. Outside the temple, on the steps of the church, facing the door, the profane person, the stranger to the sacred, is ready to cross a significant threshold, to penetrate the hidden meaning of the sacred from which he feels separated and for which he feels nostalgia.

Facing the sexual door, the profane individual prepares to love deeply. He holds the desire to transpose his sexuality to another plane than the temporal plane. This has not yet taken place but the intuition of what love could be haunts him. He stands in a waiting, exploratory stance. He discovers and practices his passions one facet at a time. He sorts them out, prepares, makes a first and then a second attempt to express his desires, is disappointed, closes, opens again. He searches, keeping both hands in the charnel clay.

During this stage, the human being is alienated from his true sexual nature—a nature that is double: Feminine and masculine, yin and yang, expansive and contracted, heart-felt and genital. He compensates his waiting, his impatience with the worship of a certain aspect of sex—reductionist, performance-related, external—rather than giving himself to the worship of femininity. Eventually, he will enter into the patience of inner work and allow himself to be tempted by intimacy. He does not yet know that the threshold he has to cross is feminine and that he will have to discover that reality...

> *An obsessional style, treating beings like things, one-upmanship, standardization and disorientation characterize modern sexuality. Sexuality ... is killed by free time, idleness, and emptiness instead of being stimulated.*
> Dr. Gerard Leleu

Jean Letschert, in Être à deux ou les traversées du couple (*Being Two or the Ins and Outs of a Couple*) speaks to us about the profane aspect of sexuality: "We see that nothing in the modern materialistic world favors a spiritual, much less sacred, notion of the relationship between a man and a woman. Horizontal and unilateral consumption of an object by a subject seems to be the most widespread relational model in our society, which is short-circuited by competition and leisure activities. Additionally, in the world of spirituality as well, the acceptance of sexuality as a reflection of the Sacred has always been a delicate and subversive question. Few in number are the adventurers of the spirit who have dared to tackle this problem head on, at the risk of being considered perverted, possessed or heretical. Sexuality that is free and sexuality that is sacred without its sole objective being procreation remains subject to blame, excommunication and exile."

For the profane person, man or woman, who has not yet discovered the sense of intimacy and the feminine aspect of the sexual energy, objects are to be fixed up, breasts are to be enlarged out of proportion, but the buttocks—not so much! Sexual activities are mechanical and love relationships utilitarian. Accent is on the *plumbing* of the sexual body, on its dysfunctions and the tricks to overcome them. It's no longer a question of working on the relationship. Stimulants are easy to find through the internet, Viagra and other avenues. Laziness wins out; the easy way is too attractive and a love relationship is too difficult to live through—too confrontational. Why go to the trouble when it's so easy to use pornography or the first person who comes along to get what you're looking for—a release of tension. What ensues is confusion, backing off, suffering, no satisfaction, lack of creativity, lack of vitality—for both sexes.

The essential core of these manifestations that cause suffering has its origin in the rejection of feminine energy and is the result of a long patriarchal moment. The solution is to be found then in the return to a devotion offered to the inner femininity. The healing path winds through the wounds inflicted on femininity—wounds in men just as well as in women.

Letting go of old wounds caused by a profane vision of sexuality helps us. We must remind ourselves of our resources and of our current sexual strengths.

The solution is to be found also in the inner work that allows a marriage of feminine and masculine energy. It's an heroic work in which, among other things, expectations are abandoned or at least calmed and in which projections, animus and anima, are rendered positive. Making our way through all our differences and through our individuality which a love relationship imposes on us, the path of return to oneself opens. We make our way to a fullness of being. This fullness is depicted by the circle in the symbols that represent the second chakra. The circle is a finite whole, integral and perfect and yet delimited by its own boundary. It contains its own space. It is a container that defines its own content. It doesn't necessarily speak to us of the place where we must be inside ourselves but instead of the life goal to be pursued... for all time!

I have done my best to say no to the absence of love, to the masquerade of love, to the exercise of love—in the sense of trying to love and to orgasm. Trying without deep feeling is repulsive to me. Sexual energy, when reduced to its strictly physical and outlet/release dimension, when isolated from its relational and heart-felt aspect, always seemed invasive to me. I never quite knew what to do about it, how to set up pathway markers around it. The experience of it was difficult and sublimating it did not interest me. No, I wanted to allow it to spread out, to flourish in desire, to become charged with all its spiritual essence, and carry me away in a rapture that would be continually renewed and would be always renewable. Life energy, the very energy that manifests in sexuality, has to ascend. Since its verticality was thwarted in me, I moved into a grey zone filled with pain and solitude. In my love relationships, the first experiences of my sexuality never ceased to come back, damaging the new relationships, searching to bring comfort—in illusion and horizontally—to the sexual tension without regard for the heart and awareness of being divine.

I did not let myself be known in my soul or in my flesh. They did not know in me either the lesser or the greater of my desires, those which made my heart dream, those which made my body tremble and sing. They did not know how to listen to my body's prayer and I hid it from them. I hid that prayer from myself, as if I were a stranger to my own story, stubbornly fleeing every abductor, ceaselessly and without awareness, perpetuating the story of the women of my family and of their sisters of misery. Today I know that prayer! It has taken all this time to understand that my sex is sacred and that my pleasure is a hymn. It has taken all this time to know to what extent my heart is breakable and that my body, in its sensual and sexual nature, is the essential manifestation of my whole being.
Passages from my diary

Cardiac or Intimate Sexuality:
The Love that is Patient

Intimacy with Oneself

Before being dual, intimacy is singular. There would exist an intimate place in each human being—a secret spot, private and deep, an inner fort, a place where all facets of existence come together. The very essence of the word intimacy refers to the concept of interiority since the Latin *intimus* is a superlative of *interior*. Current usage defines the geography of this place by giving the center of the self as pivot of support: I'm writing my intimate diary, I have a circle of intimate friends (all around me, very close to me), the intimate feeling of a betrayal.

Interesting to note that the French word for intimate is *intime*, which when read in English becomes *in time*. The notion of time introduces the idea of movement. Thanks to this play on words, we reflect on what we need to achieve in our inner life—the experience of full intimacy with oneself. Being in time, in one's inner time, being on time, up to date in one's work of introspection and of personal growth. An image appears: A person descends a spiral staircase toward a central point, coming closer and closer to the center while respecting his inner time, that is, his own rhythm. When I take the time to travel gently toward the center of myself, I enter into a place that is deeply connected to myself. Intimacy creates a state in me which resembles me and re-assembles me. Scattering is turned back on itself. In this sense, intimacy is singular before being double.

Intimacy is singular, that is, it comes about in a person for herself, in herself, and that is the essential condition of the intimacy between two people, two people who are whole, who have no need of the other person but welcome intimacy like a gift in a very full life, a life lived with happiness.

Intimacy with Another Person

> *Intimacy is the relationship within which feelings and thoughts as well as the totality of the intra-personal life of each person are revealed to the partner—they are even explored together. The lover searches out this intimacy which allows him to explore, even at the risk of being hurt, all the similarities and all the differences that exist between him and his beloved.*
> Jules Bureau

Two people who are in the process of becoming complete in themselves and who seek a feeling of fullness are ripe for experiencing a harmonious, loving relationship, unencumbered with merging spaces, those become less and less frequent. The expression *my better half* is meaningless. No body is half of what they are. A couple is composed of two people each of whom is whole.

Because solitude (in that little energetic space assigned to us and that nobody can really occupy with us) is really so trying that it gives rise in each partner to the desire of a moment, even a fleeting one, of reunion, of solidity, of loving kindness. The fact of not being able to be other than oneself, alone and unique, marvelous but limited, impels you toward a movement of union, creates an imperious need to penetrate into the world of the other person, to fuse, to discover oneself in the other person, to transcend the difference for one little moment of wonderment. In that moment, you try to dissolve the tension caused by what is missing. You try to bring into your existence what is not there but which exists in the other person with a disarming simplicity since it is his own way of being. That is the grandeur of intimacy... if we accept not to remain trapped in the illusion that we will fix loneliness and instead engage in a return to oneself. Intimacy is a round trip voyage between one heart and another in order to end up coming to rest within oneself. This final movement is the most important. Too often lovers forget themselves when with the other person.

Intimacy is an almost religious state that illuminates love, a state that opens out onto what the two partners have that is most sacred—the heart, at the same time as they anchor the heart solidly in the body and in its sexual reality.

Intimacy: A Quest for Oneself

> *Nothing is ever acquired by man—not his strength, not his weakness, not his heart.*
> Louis Aragon

Being face to face with the other person, which generates sexual desire, is experienced heart to heart in the deep feelings of the body and attempts to transcend all dichotomies. The quest for oneself is to travel, through the beloved, along one's own inner spaces until the ultimate space is reached—the core of one's being.

You discover that you are vulnerable with innumerable inner spaces to explore, to fill up, to perfect. The greater the intimacy and the more each person abandons himself/herself to what is, the less there is resistance to change and to discoveries. Even the smallest areas that are dark, mistaken or still denied, get broken down like a dike that gives way. They become what they ought to be— that is, elements that build up the masculine or the feminine in each person. The man becomes more of a man by taking on a little of the feminine from his partner, by recognizing it, by putting it in the light and by integrating it into his masculinity. And from that his masculinity doesn't feel diminished but rendered more substantial, more solid. This feminine part has always been there in him but it had never been actualized. For the woman, it is her masculine interior which undertakes the same voyage. In a homosexual couple, a similar work is possible since there is always one of the partners who is more feminine or more masculine.

Intimacy is meeting the other person and tasting his unifying energy. The evocation of the other person in oneself echoes in one's own heart which is opening—the simple thought of the other person awakens the body and butterflies begin to dance at his/her center. Love re-activates the most ancient layers of the being and brings the lovers *grown up and enlarged* to the full beauty of their being—in a breathing that is constantly renewed. Love also brings up all that does not resemble it with the intention of offering a healing. Patiently welcoming everything that hurts and enriching oneself with it, instead of trying to get rid of it, is a measure of the success of the intimacy in oneself and with the other person.

Love: Its Difficulties, Its Richness

> *Not only our relationships, but life itself brings sudden shocks and blows. Our most precious hopes collapse— that is their nature. The most unexpected marvels are within reach. That also is in their nature. By refusing to taste the bitter along with the honeyed, we are refusing to be part of the ineffable nature of love itself.*
> Brenda Shoshanna

It is always saddening to realize to what an extent the human being knows how to make obstacles to happiness. He gets bogged down in fear, resists feeling, cancels out being fully present in the body, makes the body an object, disallows the conquest of his own subjectivity, refusing to be seen and discovered. He discourages himself, sabotages himself and returns in misery to his suffering. Whereas the movement of love is one of fluidity, of suppleness, of a calling and of an opening to life. At the beginning, between the other person and oneself, what comes slipping in are all the emotions—the most beautiful as well as the most difficult ones, the greatest as well as the less noble ones—snapped up by thoughts of all sorts as many destructive ones as positive ones. At the beginning of the relationship, the mind repeats fables from the past, making each partner wander, straying away from their sacred part, the heart, which is both the receptacle and creator of love. This is the time of passionate love. Intimate love, patiently, demands that the head be silenced. It repatriates to the center of each partner the contact with the essence of things. An awareness of being awakened spreads deeply through the flesh, animated by love and by a renewed desire. It becomes anchored in the stability of each lover's identity. Lovers are bringers of love and makers of intimacy.

Desire is very far from being magic; it has to be cultivated. It goes missing after a certain time in the relationship; the partners panic and think of letting things drop. However, this absence or breakdown of desire is profitable to the love relationship. Intimacy rests on the intention of increasing desire, making it better, fuller and of becoming a stakeholder in the work of the harmonization and maturation of each of the partners in the relationship. The intention of tending towards a fullness of being instead of simply awakening, of making the sexual desire functional or even repairing it, takes into consideration what is most noble in existential becoming and in human happiness. The word *fullness* here is charged with an ontological meaning and refers to the existential search for *full being*, being totally what the human is... what each one of us has the capacity to be, to become. Don't be content with *just a little* in the domain of sexuality or in the totality of one's life. Dare to dream: *Full*, total, and perfected in one's essence and in one's sexuality. In this way, there opens into awareness the notion of the person who originates himself in the heart of his body, in the fullness of the experience of coming together with the other person—different and similar at the same time, desired and loved. There is work to be done on desire instead of letting the whole relationship drop when a moment comes where desire is absent. The first threshold to cross is to desire one's own life.

Love is inner and subjective. It is nourished by difference, by desire, by movement forward toward the other person. It depends on the happiness and the life that each of the lovers has installed in himself/herself. In this sense, love is a luxury that takes place in the life of someone who is already happy with oneself. It is neither a pill for anxiety nor a compensation for a life never been taken on. Love dreads too great a proximity, weakens in total fusion and in refusal of solitude. It only opens its wings in the big breath that allows a certain distance, in a constantly renewed respect for the loved one as well as for oneself. Love is demanding, but knows very well how to give everything to the one who knows how to love himself before anyone else.

As for sexual pleasure, it updates the impression, the illusion of eliminating the rupture in the totality of one's being and of being led back to the deep roots of this totality. The anguish of being separate and finite is calmed—for a time. The intimate meeting of two confirmed bodies gives rise to pleasure and its comforting fullness. A secret part of the being is comforted... until the next thirst.

In orgasmic pleasure, the energy often rises up right to the physical heart and tears happen spontaneously. It's often impossible to hold them back. Through the experience of orgasms that make us cry, this special taste that an open heart offers, this honey taste is discovered. We learn to come back to it. And love for the person with whom this ascending sexual energy is shared takes on more maturity, fewer projections, more acceptance of what is. This is patient love.

Vertical or Sacred Sexuality

You don't need to be a Buddhist or Tantric practitioner, you don't even need to be interested in spirituality. It's a question only of this reality: Your desire to be in the world totally, without inhibition, without fear, without anguish. The desire to be integrally available to life is enough
Daniel Odier

Here is the meaning of orgasm: Your energy, which up to now has been paralyzed, begins to melt, to enter into the unity of the universe. You become one with the trees, with the stars, with all women and all men, with the rocks, with all of nature. Just for one little moment. But, in this moment, there opens awareness of the sacred, of the All and of the One because this moment comes from the entirety of things. The orgasm is not a release of tension, it's a celebration.
Osho

Sexuality is a celebration of life itself in all the nuances of its beauty.

Thanks to the multiple facets, shadows and difficulties that it includes and to the generosity of its light, sexuality sustains the deployment of the whole being. Its humanity, which is trying and prodigious, can be married to its intangible divinity with felicity if banality and unawareness are banished. It is not a question here of sexual relationships being reduced to what can amount to a quite uncertain pleasure at a particular time. Real sexual flowering is the ability of sexual energy to circulate freely and steadily through the entire body, to raise the frequency of subtle vibrations, and to participate in the awakening of consciousness and the opening of the heart.

Sexual energy doesn't always rise up gradually—it can provoke destabilizing upsets. It awakens each energy center, illuminating the center as it passes through, and shakes the entire being with specific work. Its aim is clear and it does not brook any interference. It forges on toward the crown chakra in an effort to go beyond the head, the intellect, which it impregnates with a purifying fire. Great efforts are deployed by the ego to oppose that movement. The struggle is merciless. Life proposes and the ego resists—that's its vocation. Eventually, the ego must die to the world of illusion to which it is so attached. However the ego cannot come to that unless it has first of all been committed with all its strength and unless it has been able to express itself with all the nuances of its human color including its sexual color. The sexual color cannot be denied, neglected or mistreated.

A deep and ancient part of the life energy, therefore sexual energy, must awaken in order to finally have the possibility of engaging in its verticality, plowing with its rays through the whole body, penetrating the emotions that are lodged there and healing bodily hurts. The genital area is no longer then the center of sexual expression. The being can explore his totality— his power can be vivified and hold its own.

Kundalini is the subtle energy of the denser sexual energy. It is represented in certain religious icons of the East by a serpent biting its own tail. It is a wild energy, coiled in the confines of our immortal being, at the borders which demarcate the present life from our previous lives. It is a prisoner that is guarded by a demented and powerful dragon. It sleeps often in a dreamless sleep. It is good for it to awaken gently through an assiduous work on oneself. Several years are necessary to prepare for its arising, to then integrate its regenerative action and to accept to relinquish ecstasy for the benefit of rootedness. It takes several years to kill the dragon and find freedom of being and all the rest of life in order to make this freedom one's own. Awakened sexual energy, and its aura (the kundalini) lead more securely than anything else to... oneself. They demand that you live wisely and consciously.

During a time of the awakening of the sacred, thanks to a sexuality that tends to verticality and that possibly provokes a rising up of kundalini, a constant revisiting of our values is necessary. Sexual energy can be invasive, too much so perhaps, but when intimacy is renewed it gets recharged with new breath. Heartfelt exchanges deepen. Separation vanishes, unity re-establishes itself. I think that we can voyage from the profane to sacred intimacy but I don't think the opposite is possible. It's an initiation to which the heart must consent and which must be taken on without going back to past sexual recipes.

The opening of the heart is more important in spiritual work than the awakening of sexuality. However, the awakening of sexuality fosters the opening of the heart, sustains it and nourishes it. Sexual energy is spiritual. Erotic imagination is not contrary to the purity of the being. We need to drop the thought that all sexuality obscures the relationship with the Light and we need to allow the poetry of physical love and the initiatory mysteries of femininity to enter into us.

Passionate or intimate aspects, or patient aspects, of sexuality and of love integrate slowly over the course of passing days.

The sense of a more sacred sexuality develops. It does not necessarily involve a Tantric practice. It involves recognizing that the divine is manifested in all things and that it dwells in a happy body—open and sexual.

> *I had evolved from the genital world to a search for a more authentic intimacy. I began to tend towards a sacred sexuality. Profaning, desecrating my sex, ridiculing my body, ignoring it, were no longer options. That was no longer possible. For a long time, like many women, I had not been a woman who was looked at, desired, recognized. I had not been a known woman. This was not how I experienced my liaisons, my brief love affairs or even my very significant relationships. I had not let myself be known, known as if we had been born together. No man had been able to bring me into the world until the day of a first being seen. I don't really know if it was my seeing, or being seen by the Light, or the seeing by my husband or even if this non-temporal seeing from a loving eye was that of this new world that I was beginning to inhabit. Suddenly, I felt, deeply and from the inside, my beauty as a woman and this impression curled up in my heart for the first time. I must have been seen before but I had never really received a look of love. Had it been offered? Without a doubt... Had I deprived myself of it? Absolutely...*
> *Passage from my diary*

For an Expanded Sexuality

Breathing: The ideal exercise for harmonizing the second chakra

> *Breathing means to get moving; it's an inner choreography. Breathing has us learn about our body—its strengths, its*

limits and its potential. Learning about our body is to reposition it in reality.
Cherkaoui, Dancer and Choreographer

Breathing

Breathing is complex and simple at the same time. It is essential and can be mastered. Blood is the vehicle of the respiratory gasses. Blood that is purified by an adequate breathing and fortified by eating well facilitates the healing of physical wounds as well as emotional wounds.

Don't assume that you know how to breathe. Breathing affects the way we think and feel our life. Oxygen nourishes our brain, awakens our hearts and calms our nervous system. Breathing is the best tool for positively influencing our life force and our emotions.

Each person breathes differently. What is your respiratory imprint?

Each emotion presents a different breathing pattern. For example, tension and fear convert to superficial, rapid breathing. Busyness gives rise to short, hobbled breathing. Conscious tears and cries promote release in the breathing. Emotions of repressed anger and sadness lead to a restriction of respiratory movement. The way we breathe affects our thoughts and emotions and our way of thinking and feeling affects our breathing.

Symbolically

After each breathing cycle, the usual stop time is like a little death. The emptiness created by breathing out encourages us to want to take air in again. The body remembers this constant choice for renewal: To live. And the next breathing in is a positive response to the offer of life inherent in existence. Breathing in is really wanting the parcel of air that is offered to us, which is simply our right to life. It is knowing that we don't only breathe a mixture of oxygen, nitrogen and rare gasses but also a subtle energy of life that too often we refuse. It seems that we are created to experience life in a free way. We can choose to paddle against the current or let ourselves be carried by the wave.

Breathing unhindered is proof of the pure joy of being alive. And it is a measure of satisfying sexual relationships. The energetic circuits open through the breathing and pleasure is able to ascend and spread through the whole body.

Exercise in Conscious Breathing

For a few minutes, a few times a day: Stop, even in the middle of an engaging activity. Close your eyes and breathe, leaving out the pause at the end of breathing out and breathing in. This breathing—conscious, continuous, round—is no longer mechanical. It requires to observe the felt sense in the body and in the emotions. It calms the mind and energizes the body. The few minutes that you might think have been lost support a greater capacity for working afterwards.

This daily practice of a continuous, circular, gentle breathing facilitates increased oxygenation without leading to hyper-ventilation. Renewed awareness of life penetrating matter opens the body, clears blockages and muscular tensions, decrystallizes fear and painful memories. It prepares the way for the circulation of sexual energy. And for success with the following exercise.

Exercise during Sexual Relations

Exchange of breath

Aim: Moving toward a sacred sexuality—alone or in a couple.

The breath must be able to rise up through the open chakras.

Alone: With awareness, breathe within oneself. Let the energy, the breath, rise up through the body. This breathing prepares for the exchange with a partner. It keeps the sexual energy alive in oneself in times of celibacy.

In a couple: The exchange takes place in breathing together, at the same rhythm. This needs to be found and can be found in the slowness and attention given to the exercise. One person conducts the exercise and the other follows. Then the roles reverse.

Another way of exchanging: One person inhales the other's actual expiration; then the roles reverse in a continuous giving of one's breath and partaking of the other's breath.

Awareness is concentrated on the act of making the breath rise in oneself, even when exchanging with the other person. Allow yourself to be penetrated by the sensuality of the movement of air charged with a sexual quintessence...

In the Course of Your Daily Life

Breathe out... Sigh

Think of not blocking the breathing. Take a deep breath from time to time during the day. Breathe out completely. Sigh often.

Maintain the sense of your own sexuality in all dimensions and in all seasons of life—even when growing old and even when living without a partner. Continuing to be a sexual being is to continue to be dazzled by the beauty of the world and by the people you love. It is to continue being attentive to your whole body and its sensitivity. It is to continue being dynamic and remaining in contact with your life force. It is to continue to express yourself from the heart.

Water being the symbol par excellence of fluidity in relationships, playing with water in all its forms keeps sexuality awakened. Go to the sea often. Bathe in pure water lakes. Let the water from the shower flow along your back imagining that it is washing away the silt accumulated in your aura.

Chapter 12

Radiating

We have gone past the element earth to the element water and now we come to the element fire! Our dance continues in the passion of re-appropriating our bodies and exploring our emotions and our desires in order to make room for will, intention and action.
Anodea Judith

Fire Brings Light and Purification

Breathe deeply. Take a few big breaths and let them go completely.

Enter your belly—consciously come into contact with your inner furnace. Awaken to this very intimate, very personal energy. Place your hands on your belly (on the solar plexus: stomach, liver, pancreas/spleen) if desire moves you to do that. Be very sure that this region of your body is relaxed. The energy that you feel there is your power. This all-around, unique power is related to the sun, to heat, to combustion, to transformation and to the emotions. Breathe into your belly as you imagine a beautiful yellow sun is lighting you up inside. Your inner fire purifies you, detoxifies you. It gives you the impetus to express yourself in the world, to radiate, to assert this power that is fully yours.

Become aware of the emotions that sometimes invade you or the ones that you enjoy the most. Relax in the presence of these emotions—without judgment, without criticism. Ask your emotional being and ask the flame burning inside you to transform all feeling and all passion into strength, strength of being, strength of action. Embrace everything that stirs in you, everything that makes you alive and gets you moving. Even embrace what opposes your first impulse and tries to immobilize you. Embrace the light and the shadows; embrace the days gone by and those to come. Embrace the difficult nights and the nights of enlightening dreams. Let go of the past and of any preoccupation with the future. Let your heart burn with love for today's day.

Wish for laughter and tears and anger and joy... Honor all your emotions, the most beautiful ones and the most difficult ones.

Let your awareness extend into the guts of the earth, into the deepest fire of life, one and indestructible. Starting from this alliance with the center of the earth, let your awareness move up to the center of yourself charged with telluric fire, charged with the intention of allowing your authentic being to radiate through the entire universe.

Breathe in, breathe out, breathe in, breathe out...

Express your gratitude for this fire that inhabits you and burns your fears and your suffering to a cinder. Express your gratitude for the sun which lights the earth, produces food and warms your heart. Express your gratitude for the talents that have developed in you. Give thanks... give thanks! With a full letting go!

The Fire of the Emotions

Your dance with life is deployed over time and with the heart that you put into this work. The most recent chapters have perhaps made you more capable of reclaiming your relationship with Mother Earth and no doubt you have contributed to her healing. You have explored certain emotions as well as your rapport with other sexual beings. The first three chakras form a physical, temporal trilogy: Root chakra, sacred chakra, and solar plexus. In exploring these very human territories, you seek to elevate yourself more and more toward a sacred, subtle state, one that leads to the divine inside of you. For the moment you are looking outward, in the direction of a career choice, for professional advancement, expressing and honing your talents to pursue new knowledge and experience. Life is expanding in you and your inner fire is well stoked.

Being better acquainted with your desires and with your life plan, you are ready to be precise about your intention for life and for acting with regard to your radiating in the world and your service to humanity. Radiating what? Who is radiating and how? For whom? What are your intentions?

What emotions do you still have difficulty with? Which are the ones you enjoy the most? Which are the ones that bother you the most?

Are there unresolved situations in your life that maintain certain paralyzing emotions like unexpressed hurt, unconsumed anger, irrational fears? Are you feeling an impression of separation or isolation? Are you fairly happy working professionally or is it hard? Is your social life satisfying?

What emotions have you experienced, are you experiencing, in relation to your work or your studies? Do you see a connection with unresolved situations in your immediate family? In your extended family?

If you were afraid, if you were feeling vulnerable in the past, do you feel more comfortable now, safer in your life surroundings or your work surroundings? What would it take to feel safer and more open if that has not already been done?

Is your professional position at the level you hoped for? What do you need to work on to come to full professional deployment?

What connections are you making between what you are experiencing at work and what you are experiencing in other emotional environments.

Place of Existence

What are the most precious inner qualities that are now yours?

The first chakra refers to the energetic location that we occupy on the earth. It's our most precious birthright. This chakra demarcates the place we come back to in the electromagnetic grid that forms a trellis around the earth. Our date of birth informs us about the nature of our connection with humanity, defines several parameters about our life and nourishes a strong feeling of belonging.

The third chakra refers to a functional place of existence. It is also energetic but specifically it facilitates our accomplishments at all levels of our existence, particularly on the professional level.

This functional place of existence almost always manifested starting in childhood or sometimes a little later. It defines our talents and our affinities with our life mission. This place must be recognized so we can begin to affirm ourselves and love ourselves in the human labors that are offered for us to accomplish. Our date of birth indicates our nature and our potential. Our place of existence offers us the means to fulfill ourselves. Revealed during childhood, it is to be found at certain turning points in life if it hasn't been present all along.

For example, being a sports person, loving your engagement in sports is one thing, being a skilled athlete is another. A place of existence is built through perfecting an art, a sport or any other talent or aptitude. The competence and excellence acquired open a path for the manifestation of oneself in the external world. A gift for music, a good head for mathematics, the love of literature, an aptitude for teaching or practicing the art of taking care of others, to name only a few avenues of expression, can constitute the raw material of a place of existence. What is developed over numerous hours of practice has the power of being deployed in one's professional life as a place of existence. It's not just a matter of talents but of an opening in our lives where we come into touch with our profound essence. Somewhat as though our soul was busying itself to have us know what service orientation it had planned for us.

What is your place of existence?

As for me, academic excellence throughout my schooling constituted my place of existence and it was through a late return to university studies that I was able to manifest my life mission.

Returning to School: An Example

My forties ended for me on a rather sad note and prospects for my fifties looked hard. I felt empty, without desire, without direction and without effective accompaniment. Like my inner vision, my sight was changing even though I did not yet know that my eyes were preparing to cover over almost completely. However, in my travel bag, precious knowledge and experience—very definitely real—were still there, camouflaged in the folds of the worn-out leather.

And then, an angel passed my way... The heavens remembered me without my having prayed and one of its messengers touched my shoulder to awaken me. Several years ago, I would have been embarrassed to recount the event this way. I would have termed it childish. But having lived through a tangible experience of the divine, I no longer speak of illusion or faith,

I speak of an intimate reality. Remaining silent about it would be to deny myself.

That day, I received a letter from the university telling me that it was time to register for the last courses necessary for my first cycle diploma. I needed to reply in the affirmative otherwise my file would be closed and I would have to ask to enroll again with all the required procedures and costs to open a new file if I decided to complete my studies at a later time. I had firmly decided that I would never return to university but I knew, because of that hand on my shoulder, that I had to say yes. I knew it with certainty even if I didn't understand the reasons why the first threshold to cross towards freedom were to take me into the academic world. Blind and immediate acceptance was the only valid response for my soul.

A year later, I decided in the same way to pursuit a master's degree in sexology. An angel, the same one as the year before, the one who engages in reflection within me and whom I sometimes call my deep intuition, using a discreet but firm and clearly perceptible gesture, urged me to register for the program in clinical sexology even though I had stated that I would never do that. I must be really hard headed because, faced with this obvious decision, I still resisted and took detours. In fact, I registered first of all for a masters in research with all kinds of justifications for not following the therapy route which was essentially my path. The angel was obliged to come round again and, showing great patience, repeated his message: "I ought to register in clinical not research!" I laughed at myself. I had acted so seriously.

I remember so clearly walking on the rue St. Denis, near the Carré St. Louis in beautiful August sunshine. I came to a stop for a few seconds, seized by a certainty and incredulous: "It's too late. Courses begin next week. The system doesn't work like that, and so on." The angel insisted. I tried for late registration and I was accepted...

With practical things I encountered no difficulty. On the contrary, everything fell into place to facilitate what needed to be done and I received excellent support from several people at the university and from my immediate entourage. The inspiration to complete my studies in sexology was a grounding one for me. I had to place my feet on the ground with more acceptance. I had to embrace the energetic space that had belonged to me since my birth but which I had not managed to integrate with all my strength and all my awareness. I had to awaken, that is, to awaken once again to my life and find a way of unlocking myself, of opening my wings, and rising up to my heights. I was being called to distill my knowledge, to give back what I had received, acquired and understood. The seeds deposited in the terrain of my soul during inner work, accomplished during my years of therapy and in spiritual communities, was getting ready to expand outward. Finishing up my study project responded to several needs. Among others, completing my studies for the second cycle indirectly contributed to opening me to mediumship by leading me back to the center of myself and allowing me to develop in professional and intellectual arenas.

In addition, in the course of producing essays during my studies and an important report of activities that had to be drafted, my writing and my ability to write in a sustained way improved. I learned how to organize my thoughts better and how to make them accessible. My talent made a quantum leap through the many pages I had to write. I managed to discipline my expectations as well as my desire for perfection. It is thanks to my university studies that this book exists. It is what it is. It expresses, unreservedly, all that I am at this moment. Thanks to these studies, I felt sufficiently competent to offer training in mediumship and that allowed me to deepen my work with the Light.

On the wall of my therapy office there is enthroned now this sheet of blue and white paper which affirms that I know what I'm doing even if it says nothing about who I am. It's incredible how my words find their way more easily to those who consult me thanks to that paper. Every day, it reminds me that my words have value as inspiration and guidance. I remember now a truth that I had forgotten: "I'm worth my weight in gold." No longer forgetting that truth, my work really begins to take off, my words are charged with a deep meaning, my interventions become simpler and more intuitive. I offer them with more humanity. *Miracles* don't necessarily happen, but love is always present.

The academic world and the excellence that I exhibited in it occupied a big place in my childhood. They had to be reconstructed and reappear on my spiritual journey. I offered incredible resistance to this necessity; but life, no matter how unaware we are, has more than one trick up its sleeve to bring us back to a place of existence that was shown to be essential in childhood. Either there is continuity or there is a return to values that have brought about the first grounding—that have demarcated and nuanced the energetic territory to be occupied among humans. For the same reason, my relationship with nature, especially in walking, unfurled once again in my fifties and I came to really feel at home on the earth.

I understood that my identity and my value in this existence had been put in doubt by family circumstances. These circumstances were not better or worse than any others but they had a specific impact. This impact manifested in the form of doubt. This doubt was part of how I needed to learn an inner ease in relation to my place of existence. This is how it came about that I went back to school in my fifties.

The Ego, the I, and the Self

> *Our nature includes the full range of human color. When, through spiritual idealism, we want to leave the dark behind, we lose track of the light.*
> Daniel Odier

The poor ego—how rejected it is in the spiritual world!

I dare to affirm that without an ego that is recognized, worked upon and fortified, there is no authentic spiritual awakening— not in the West in any case. I don't deny that turning to eastern spiritual practices that advocate abandoning the ego can be beneficial. But we must adapt them to who we are and not adapt ourselves to them. For centuries, we have been living differently. Our roots have been nourished in a different earth and our inner landscape offers a very distinct perspective. East enriches West and vice versa. They can be married but not merged; their richness resides in their specificities.

Ego generally designates the representation of oneself: Identity, sexual identity, gender, profession, social status, and the roles of family, society and culture. More specifically, the ego is constructed with objects that we place in our lives and which end up defining the person we are or that we believe ourselves to be. The ego, in a necessary movement, cultivates these objects as well as the illusion that they define us completely. The ego hangs on to the mirroring of these illusions and makes sure that others only see Mr. Ego in his Sunday best—whatever the price that the heart may have to pay for that.

The ego ensures the mechanics of survival and defense in the face of danger, whether it's real—such as a car bearing down on us—or whether it's less tangible such as someone harassing us. The ego is the one that panics when life or identity are threatened. The *I* is the part of the psyche that knows what to do and how to properly handle the errors and limits of the ego and the attacks that it believes it is the victim of. In an era when our survival is no longer put in question on a daily basis, the attention of the human being is turned toward mechanisms of psychological defense. Because it is more available, the attention is also turned toward the construction of its own center and toward the radiating of this center into the world. We now have the possibility and the time to be at the service of humanity and of the divine. It is the *I*, the ego's twin, that takes on this service by crafting its talents, its desires and its aspirations.

The *I* is an ego that has been worked on, a bridge erected between the shadow and the light of our being. It acts as a possible way of reaching our divine nature. A real *I* expresses itself through a more authentic, more integrated personality. It is freed from the tyranny of the ego which fades away but never dies. Like the moon in the daytime, only a feeble glow remains but it does not disappear completely. The *I* is the essential perfume of oneself.

> ... attacking the ego is a misguided way of attacking yourself. Destroying the ego serves no purpose even if it were doable. It is essential to keep your creative machinery intact. When you take away its ugly, fearful, violent dreams, the ego loses its ugliness, its fear and its violence. It takes its natural place in the mystery.
> Deepak Chopra

The collected *I* flows from an inner sense of self, one that is less separate and is in the process of reuniting and developing positively. It supports a forward movement that is more balanced and even allows the awakening of a more rooted consciousness. The human often has no idea that his many busy thoughts are not essential to him and do not lead to Truth. The heart, in its expression of love, irrigates the movement of inner reunion. This reunion cannot take place without the recognition of the initial division, or without what the ego knows. Spiritual work is often conducted too soon and too quickly and the personality can find itself dispersed to the periphery—even fragmented. Self-esteem brings us back to a rightful measure of being. It assembles all pieces of the self, the least glorious as well as the most luminous.

In the field of modern spirituality and the transpersonal, the ego is distinguished from the Self (the higher *I*, the higher self). The ego is sometimes considered as the foundation of the personality, in particular in psychology, and sometimes as a hindrance to our personal development, notably in spirituality. Certain spiritual circles cultivate the following concept: *If I were truly awakened, I would no longer experience emotions. I would no longer ever be sad or angry because I would know that all is one and eternal.* In fact, nothing is separated from anything. Sadness, for example, is one with what we could call the Truth. But, sadness that originates from an illusion doesn't need to be cultivated. From the moment that illusion attenuates and reality appears to us as it is, sadness is pure and full. It is true and it forms an integral part of human nature—to be honored. It is part of the ego, the *I*, and the Self. Just like the other emotions.

There is the ego and then the *I* which is like a fortified, purified ego. There is the heart, which has had a chance to open through work on the ego. During the long journey from the ego to the *I* to the Self, the heart nourishes each step forward. According to Jung, the Self then would be the integration of all parts of the personality allied with the soul, the inner divine.

Working from the ego toward the *I* and then the Self is done by illuminating the shadow. It involves numerous awakenings while allowing our illusions and our desires to die. We travel through the negative of our masculinity and our femininity, the negative of the high and the low, of the right and the left, so that we might discover a way of making them positive, of marrying our dualities, our oppositions. The *I*, through reconquering all its pieces—rejected, unloved, hidden, unrecognized—leads back to the heart, and then to the Self.

> *Work on the ego, on the I... calls on us to die to emotional and sentimental love that has not visited any divine intelligence. It invites us to rise again to divine love.*
> Annick de Souzenelle

For a Greater Emotional Balance

> *Being in permanent movement on all levels contributes significantly to our wellbeing.*
> Dr. Jan Chozen Bays

Eating healthily and with full awareness: the ideal exercise supporting the harmonizing of the third chakra

The solar plexus is about the assimilation of all food: Material, emotional, cultural, psychological, human, celestial, familial, gregarious, divine and others. It's about assimilating all that is received in order to be able to give back to the world a richness of being and radiating.

Eating, digesting, assimilating in full awareness is a work to be conducted so that emotions are nourishing and not destructive.

Ultimately, we need to understand that all food that is *distorted* in its nature cannot have beneficial effects. We need to develop the intention of nourishing ourselves as healthily as possible on all levels.

Develop your felt sense for food

Sit down at a table that has been set with:

A pitcher of water on which is written the word *thanks*

A little plate with some white bread, another with some whole grain bread

A plate of green or red grapes

Exercise description

Drink a little water between each movement if you feel the need.

First movement:

- Bread: Taste the white bread, taste the whole grain bread. Observations: Is one better than the other? How? Really get what it is.

Second movement:

- Pick up the white bread and bless it: Thank the animals that have given their milk. Thank the wheat, ask forgiveness for the bad treatment that has been inflicted on it. Give thanks for the work of all the people who brought this bread to your table. Do the same for the whole grain bread.

Taste once again. Take time to thank. Take time to smell, taste, savor. Observe and compare the two movements, before and after.

Third movement:

- Taste a grape. Observe its taste in the mouth.

- Eat another grape, one little mouthful at a time while giving thanks.

- Ask forgiveness for the bad treatment inflicted on the grape, compromising its natural condition. Smell, taste, savor. Offer it to the divine in yourself, to the highest part. The single grape becomes an entire meal; it fills a void. It has been transformed by a grateful attitude. Gratitude transforms automatisms into attention and awareness.

Offering love and gratitude to food is the same as offering love and gratitude to yourself. This exercise can be done with any food at all. For example, if you don't eat gluten, choose something other than bread.

In the Course of your Daily Life

Eating from a bowl

In September 2012, I published this message on my blog: "For some time now, I have been eating from a bowl... a beautiful bowl about six inches in diameter and not too deep. It's wonderful. The idea of eating in a bowl is to do it with greater awareness. The roundness of the bowl brings concentration to what you are seeing and what you are doing. Right away I am eating more slowly and with more attention. Clearly, the slowness means eating less without trying. It is easier also to add less salt, tamari, fruit ketchup, sauce or salad dressing!

"The next stage in this exercise is to eat one type of food at a time, the fish or the rice first, vegetables afterward, salad last or first depending on my mood. I manage it sometimes—not always. Eaten separately, each separate food releases all its flavor and becomes a meal in itself. At the beginning—and that's where I'm still at—you can fill your bowl as often as you want. Another stage would be to simplify the meals further and to eat only one type of food at each meal and to fill your bowl only once. I don't know if I'm going to make it that far. But at the moment, I feel a great pleasure in experimenting with various ways of nourishing myself. My body seems very happy too. And all this happens without effort, without discipline and without guilt.

"Sometimes I may eat alone because my family is busy elsewhere and I like to eat in silence without music or reading, bringing great attention to each mouthful brought to my mouth and to the chewing. I feel satisfied quickly and I am no longer hungry for several hours. And then, if I'm hungry once again, I eat another bowl—always in silence. There is no restriction, only complete pleasure.

"Eating becomes a sacred movement, a recognition of the abundance offered by Mother Earth and a clear awareness of my body's needs for quality food.

"Eating becomes a prayer."

Since that time I have continued to eat from a bowl... I now have a great variety of bowls of all colors and shapes. Generally I eat with more awareness but the attitude needs always to be worked on. It's very easy to fall back into bad habits even after two years! I don't get discouraged—I'm getting there. The great pleasure of eating simply is gradually becoming part of me and is stimulating me. I don't need to develop any discipline. I need only to welcome in the happiness...

Chapter 13

Loving

Can the humblest earthly object become the journey, the wine of ecstasy, when it is observed through the inner source?
Marianne Dubois

The Source

Can the most unnoticed person become the nectar of ecstasy when embraced with a tender and confirming look from the source inside oneself, by eyes that are awakened to true love?

The body is the container, the vehicle. The soul is the inspiration. Love is the living source. Life is the manifestation. Tenderness, love, healing, relationship with what is real, infused with the divine, are the attributes of the heart.

The settling down and the calming of emotional states are a long process. The levels of understanding and work are multiple and diverse. I took my time resolving the wars that were waged in my inner world. I don't believe in flying above the darkness to arrive at the light, in ignoring the battles in order to conquer peace. I don't believe in rising above the human level but instead I believe of plunging in, body and soul. I think what's needed is a gestation time for our inner resources within the shadow of things and even within the shadow of our heart, confused by allegations from the ego. It's a long trek but the emergence of clarity, at the end of the tunnel, is unforgettable.

Earth called us and we came. We have invested the world and its materiality in a movement that tends toward completion but will never quite end even though the heart opens to the spirit and to the immensity of life. The heart opens and closes—that is its law. It opens once again and closes but is not as closed as the first time. It continues to dilate without locking itself down at the slightest fear. That is its strength. It breathes, breathing in, breathing out... breathing in, breathing out... opening, closing. It cannot stay gaping open—that would be its death.

The touch of the divine is always at the level of the heart,
and from the heart the whole being is touched. I know
that now!
Passage from my diary

Being in the Heart: A Meditation of Love

Your mantra for this meditation: I love and I am loved!

Take a few deep breaths. Breathe out completely each time. Your tongue is relaxed in your mouth. Your jaws are unclenched. Relax the nape of your neck with a few gentle movements. Let your shoulders soften, let your heart offer itself up, let your body's verticality settle in.

Let the air penetrate silently into your lungs. For this to happen, the throat must be completely relaxed and the intention of being in your heart must be clear and direct. Silence is the sole presence within you. All distraction moves away from this inner space which is dense and yet ethereal. There is nothing but an infinitesimal vibration, like a very light breeze that envelops you and subtly penetrates you without any apparent movement.

Listen to the silence in yourself. Feel this silence speak to you of love. Let yourself be cradled by a vibration that leads you a little closer to the sacred space of the heart. The matrix of the heart gives you a new impulse toward yourself and toward an higher energy.

Imagine that you could, from inside, turn your eyes toward your physical heart. What is also there in that place is the heart-center, the energetic heart in all its splendor and all its simplicity. Feel the beating of your heart. Your life has been gently beating for so long, and will continue for so long.

Breathe in, breathe out, breathe in, breathe out...

Think of making these words part of your inner core: "I am Love and I have faith in the love of the divine for me."

Express your gratitude for the air that you breathe and for the love that inhabits you. Give thanks for the love that you have to give and for the love that you receive at every moment. Give thanks... Give thanks! In full relaxation!

Let the sacred sound of OM call the love of your Guides to you. Let its sound breathe into you a renewed respect for this life in you, around you, everywhere, this immense and magnificent life maintained by the breath of love. Give thanks for the presence and support of the Beings of Light.

The Heart-Center

> *Its infinitesimally faint and continuous trembling is your*
> *own nature.*
> Daniel Odier

The organ heart rests in the middle of the chest and is looking left. The subtle heart, called the heart-center or the heart chakra, is situated directly underneath the sternum. It is located then right in the middle of the body, half way between left and right, between the upper and the lower chakras. It looks straight ahead.

From its position and from its real nature, it is the bridge that connects polarities, officiating at the marriage of all the dualities that confront each other in us. The fluid of the heart is love and its glandular manifestation is represented energetically by tears. We cry just as much from joy as from hurt.

The heart-center is the object of a lot of attention. Often, the perception of its primary role is lost in a labyrinth of metaphysical considerations, which are sometimes not well rooted. And the word heart in all of its unifying and healing reality is often debased. In fact, the heart does not stand there unique and grandiose at the center of life. Instead it is supported by a whole edifice of human substance, which cannot be neglected. Otherwise, the heart wanders off and love is dislodged from the place where the energies of the higher and lower chakras are harmonized, where polarities diminish and where opposites cease to oppose each other. If love shifts onto consumables or intoxicants or even to another person in an attempt to fuse with that person, union becomes impossible. Loving someone else or loving life is first of all to love oneself.

The love of oneself means having the courage to listen to the spiritual messages and counsels transmitted through the channel of the heart.

The heart-center teaches us what compassion is. It impregnates our ways of being and doing with a loving dimension of oneself, of others, of trials and suffering, of joie de vivre and happiness in serving humanity. It gives weight to our spiritual reality. The heart both divides and reunites. Because it divides it is able to reunite.

It is the chakra that breathes the most. It opens and closes constantly given its position between the lungs. Work on oneself calls us to experience this dynamic rhythm as harmoniously as possible: Closing/opening, taking hold/letting go, fear/confidence, descending/ascending, joy/sadness.

The heart chakra corresponds to the causal body which opens onto the recapitulation of all of our previous lives. It illuminates our cellular memory and already projects our attention on the future, an attention freed of all expectation. The heart then is life itself in its duration. The harmonization of this chakra or of the reality of the heart is carried out by love. All our past lives and even future lives assemble in the heart to be honored, loved and healed.

Mark Nepo states that "We are all born with a clear space inside us which is not inhabited by regrets or expectations, which has neither ambition or embarrassment, and which is free of all fear or anxiety. It is a primal space where divine grace first touched us." We must therefore provide for the care of our heart with attention and constancy.

The heart-center is also the chakra of the deep transformation of the human into a being who is divinely human. It presides over the journey from having to being. When the heart opens, struggles of opposition are in the process of being resolved. Desire and aggression, terror and fear are destroyed because in the heart the ego is no longer important. The sense of self is deployed in a movement of unity and elevation. The ego no longer imposes its rules, memories and projections. They are transcended by the heart. The ego, regenerated by the love of self, lets go of its attachment to its wounds and to its accusations directed at designated henchmen. It is no longer mistaken about its true nature, it ceases to see itself as a victim of all and sundry and it becomes responsible for itself. Love pacifies the ego.

Opening to the world and to others with love: The question here is no longer, *I cannot love others because I have not been loved.* It becomes, *How can I love others?*

Say Yes, Say Thank You

Say yes to the divine. Say yes to yourself. Say yes to your life mission. Just say yes. Saying yes to the divine is to say yes to the totality of life, to your body, to your humanity. Stop being lukewarm, stop believing in your fears, get moving on the road that is open in front of you, wherever it may lead. Engage in an act of love for yourself, for someone else, for humanity, for the Earth.

The act of love is opposed to fictitious, conditional, egoistic love: "I love you on the condition that... I love you but I don't want to make concrete efforts to facilitate your happiness. I love you because you are mine."

Say instead: "I love you and I show it in practical terms. I love myself and I take care of myself. I love myself and I say yes to my needs and to my aspirations. I love humanity and the earth. I also engage in social, ecological or philanthropic action as an act of love."

Saying yes is to take life in your arms and thank it for everything. Saying yes is affirming your happiness. It is moving towards another person, a person who has given you something, some love. Tell her how the offer was received, declaring the joy created by her gift, going so far as to announce your gratitude— solemnly, manifestly. All of that. All the nuances of thanks are to be explored, expressed. Much more, they are to be shouted loud and clear.

It's gratitude, even in small amounts, that opens the heart, not the love received. And especially not passionate, transitory love which creates turmoil in the heart and tends to frighten it, creating more wounds, bringing on a new closing of the heart or fostering a closing that has already been established. Love is the state we enter into by expressing our gratitude.

Try this: Imagine a person who makes you suffer a lot or who made you suffer deeply in the past. Give thanks for the presence of this person in your life, for what you think are hurtful actions. Understand why it is possible that this suffering could be redeeming or evolutionary for you. How did the redeeming happen? How did his actions, even sometimes violent, constitute the humus for your transformation? Thank this person. How do you feel?

Say thanks, recognize—which means to know once again—the perfection and the abundance that are already established in your life. Don't try to find or fabricate a perfection where it cannot exist, but re-cognize it where it already exists. Gratitude is a tool of inner relaxation, of opening to the essential in oneself. It lightens, nourishes. It unfolds, cuts away the wounds of rejection.

In Order to Open the Heart

Healing wounds of the heart: Ideal exercise allowing harmonization of the heart chakra

At the heart of our being, having identified the causes of our ills and our hurts, we express what remains from our past. We seek to heal that and to visualize confidently a beneficent future.

The direction of the inner work is double.

Toward the past:

The movement toward redemption of our bodies and of our emotional lives moves on from intimate expression to causality. In other words, in the present, express things—barriers, behaviors—which come to you from the past. You must discover their causes in order to transform the present. Knowledge of wounds from the past—what remains of them in your actual life and in your body—is the first step toward liberation. But... we need to ask ourselves if we really want to experience a healing in relation to old wounds or are we too attached to our status as a victim?

Wounds happened creating fears in relation to the pursuit of our lives and caused suffering. This suffering is real even if the ego busies itself by inflating it. Unhealed wounds drain our creative energy and takes up room in our psyche in the present. They dislodges compassion and replaces it with bitterness. Because they still produces breaks and pain, we need to attend to them.

Toward the future:

Actualizing ourselves by maturing the expression of what we know of our inner world leads to divine will. Once we have recognized, named, and healed old wounds, abandoning oneself to divine will makes possible a return to the present and to the creative expression of a future offered in all confidence to the sacredness of life.

Slowly, thanks to our inner work, we are healing our heart more and more and we are moving forward with more assurance toward our future.

Here is **an exercise** that can accelerate any healing process. It's a matter of revisiting wounds that are:

... in your roots—inherited from our ancestors, and passing by way of our conception, our gestation, our birth, and our childhood.

... in your masculinity—in our masculine being and through the masculine (father, brother, son, partner, teacher, boss, work, professional shortcomings).

... in your past—former lives, distant past or recent past.

... in your femininity—in our feminine being or through the feminine (mother, sister, daughter, partner, teacher, creativity, the body—its sexuality and health).

... in your relationship with the divine—elevation and the desire for elevation.

As a final step: Take a look at your future and at the fears that it can generate.

What to do and How to do it:

First movement:

Reflection on the core wounds that happened in:

- your roots, below, under our feet

- your masculine being, to the right

- your past, behind us

- your feminine being, to the left

- your desire for elevation, above the head

Choose a wound for each one of these emotional locations

Second movement:

Stand, settling into a calming verticality. The eyes are closed. The breathing is relaxed and conscious. The body is going to rotate around its axis in order to be positioned facing the symbolic locations of each of the wounds chosen in the first movement. For the wound associated with your roots, reach down with both arms and bring the essence of the wound into your heart by physically bringing your hands to your heart. Rotate your body 90 degrees to the right and reach straight forward and bring the essence of the wound associated with your masculine being into your heart. Repeat the process for the wounds associated with your past and your feminine being. Finally, rotate the body back to the starting position, reach up over your head and bring the essence of the wound associated with the desire for elevation into your heart—when bringing the wounds into the heart, invoke an intention of healing then open the arms returning to the universe the memory of these wounds in a burst of *letting go*.

Third movement:

At the end of the exercise, in full confidence, take one step forward toward the future. Extend your arms out in front of you to take hold of the future and bring it into your heart.

Thanks to the process of the healing of past and present wounds, fears dissolve. The desires and dreams that you no longer believed in become feasible projects. In the future, there will be no open wounds, just scars.

It is strongly recommended that you write down your process. You can repeat this exercise as often as you want choosing different wounds each time.

In the Course of Your Daily Life

Crying and Laughing

The opening of the heart is always accompanied by tears of sadness, of joy or of liberation. Don't we say, for example: *Laugh till you cry. Tears of joy. Cry your heart out.* The heart cries for the past, cries for all that is not like love. The heart cries as it opens.

The heart opens while crying and also while laughing. Laugh as often as you can, about everything and about nothing. Breathe the light. Keep the heart open as you breathe... breathe light. Imagine your breath as a very pale blue light that unifies you with the Light. Channeling is practiced with the heart completely open. Otherwise, power plays are too hurtful for the client. The same is true in daily life: Live your life each day from the heart not waiting for any particular moment to open it up.

Chapter 14

Communicating

While the bird with the secret is singing in our ears, we are groping blindly, looking for the profile of the words, trying to turn their meaning into stones in our hands, but, not having heard the bird, we lose our access to the world.
Alejandro Jodorowsky

Alone with others

"Yesterday, I put a book, a juice and a salad in my bag and went walking in my favorite park in Outremont, looking for a free bench.

"As soon as I entered the park, I was stunned by the scene that lay before me. On one side, children were playing all together in the little fenced-in sand garden. Laughter and roars of pleasure beaconed to me from the street well in advance of my arrival. On the other side, a great solitude... About twenty benches, more perhaps, all occupied by people alone, silent, their noses in a book or newspaper, heads bent—no offering being made to the sun. A few people were spread out on blankets, as singles or couples, all of them also silent. I slowly approached the only unoccupied bench that I had picked out from the other side of all this solitude. I really tried to attract a few glances—I would have smiled or offered a greeting with even a discreet movement of the head. I didn't encounter a single glance, not one head was raised as I passed by. I knew that if I had been suffering I would not have received any more attention than I did. On the contrary, the pain of other people turns heads away more surely than does joy.

"I took a seat wondering about this urban spectacle. It was familiar. Resigned to it, I took out my salad, my apple juice and my book. Alone, I read and had my meal—without any discomfort, without any joy, escaping into the imaginary world of my book and without any contact with those around me, any of whom I could have spoken to.

"Today, I feel regret. I regret not having said hello to people as I passed them even if they didn't look at me. I feel regret but does that help? Why did I too remain silent? I don't know... I only know that habit and resignation eat away at one's wings more surely than solitude does..."

I wrote this message in my blog at the end of March 2012 on a day that heralded early spring. Since then, things have changed a lot. People are no longer alone with their head in a book or a newspaper. Instead they are alone at their end of a phone line or with their head bent over their tablet! I deplore this more and more common spectacle. Not only are people more and more alone but also children are in the process of becoming even more alone than their parents or guardians. The solitude of babies in the park goes right to my heart. The adult is nearby, but glued to a cell phone, pushing the swing without even a glance—no contact at all with the child. He or she may burst out laughing or be talking animatedly with someone located miles away while the child, the least important thing present, is being pushed on a swing.

Communicating is no longer tasty. The new technologies make daily life easier, definitely, but they get in the way of our intimacy. Is there a part of our hearts that is still available for real communication?

Communication, Sacred Listening, Sacred Words

Knowing how to listen in density teaches us to hear and understand the subtle.

The opening of the fifth chakra allows us to move upward toward divine will, to accept that will and to manifest it. The fifth chakra, the throat chakra, is especially important in conducting a communication in channeling because, beyond the words, there is a subtle vibratory message—as there is in any relationship. For the message to be luminous in the given moment or for it to be really loving with those close to us in our daily life, we need to practice listening while honoring the silence, adapting what we say and harmonizing it with *what is*. The transmission of an elevated vibration through channeling or through words of love spoken in an intimate relationship must be prepared at every moment of every day.

Having access to the vibratory message of every individual with whom we come into close contact—whether in the workplace, in channeling, in a therapeutic relationship, in an intimate relationship or in society—is a security guarantee. Listening to the silence brings us to knowing the other person. Who is it I am in contact with? Do I know how to decipher what is not said, or how to go beyond appearances? Up to what point are the words exchanged in a first meeting sincere? Up to what point are the words of a medium or a channeler whom I consult charged with a vibration of love? Does love shine through in the voice of the therapist I consult, in the voice of the person saying he loves me, or in my voice when I love?

Sacred listening

The throat is able to enter into resonance with the other chakras and with other people as long as it is able to listen to them without interference. The throat is receptive to everything that is heard from others and from oneself. This is how it can construct, structure and transmit messages from our intimate world and from our world of light in channeling if that is what we intend (whether pure or not!). It reworks the defining elements from the other chakras, making from them a coherent and transmittable whole. Everything that is felt in the first chakra, shared with the second chakra, elaborated and sensed in third chakra, and which bathes in the love of an open heart must be communicated using appropriate sounds and words so that through that process, life is nourished in us.

The Larousse French dictionary tells us that resonance has the property of increasing the duration and intensity of a sound—that it is an effect, an amplified echo, produced in the mind or the heart (yes, yes—even the dictionary can be poetic!). And that resonance is the increase in the amplitude of an oscillation under the influence of periodic impulses from a neighboring frequency.

I would add that it is the ability to repeat a sound as it was heard or to respond to it with the same tonality. For example, a stringed instrument in a room will begin to vibrate when a person begins to play another stringed instrument in the same room. For this to take place, the instrument must be well tuned. This is what happens during a trance induction: The channeler, through his own body, enters into resonance with the person consulting her. Her body is the instrument she is working with. In order to translate an inner music as accurately as possible, the body must be well tuned. This is also true for all aspects of one's life.

> *Born from the Great Divine Silence, Man can only return to this silence when he becomes capable of perceiving it, because Man only speaks to the extent that he hears. He grows only within the limits of his range of hearing. His words are the expression of his evolution. The one verifies the other. Both are a function of his listening.*
> Annick de Souzenelle

Ears are not the only means of hearing. Deaf people, for example, *hear* or sense the vibrations of the music through their body. In channeling, the integrity of the luminous message depends on the listening brought to the other person's vibration and depends also on listening to one's own inner silence. Then, in this movement of sacred listening, the Light makes its song heard thanks to the ether. This enigmatic element is paired in fact with the throat chakra.

The silence is as important as the words since it is a creative action just as the listening is. Silence, listening, and words have to be in harmony. The purification of the thoughts and the intention in the communication is as important as the communication itself. Being rooted in the human is a guarantee of this purification.

The ears, that we bend in an upward movement so we can more fully grasp the person's words or the words of the divine, reflect the feet and the kidneys and participate in the same creative energy. Annick de Souzenelle in *Le symbolisme du corps humain (The Symbolism of the Human Body)* establishes a parallel between the symbolic aspect of the feet (rootedness), the aspect of the kidneys (the life force necessary for accomplishing something), and the aspect of the ears (listening). She points out that all have the same form—that of a seed, the creator of life.

The heart of every human being harbors all the vibrations needed for the evolution of his soul. The soul chooses a particular existence and a given personality at a specific moment. It is then our duty to hear the totality of one's own life and to express it with awareness. Often, this ultimate expression is preceded by a constriction, a crisis, an existential ordeal. Hearing is to become aware of the wound buried in the complaint of an individual, the wound that opens the human heart to its destiny.

I listen for my soul's murmur, for the sacred in my life, therefore I hear. The soul is difficult to hear. It only murmurs so that we have to bend our ear. However, in the tumult of our western lives, listening is rare and many secrets are lost.

We know a machine is working well by relying on the sound it makes. In the same way, the message offered by a channeler is *positive* if the tone of the voice is harmonious and loving.

Sacred words

In beginning, or continuing, to open the throat chakra, it is absolutely necessary to maintain a healthy relationship with reality and with truth. The question is knowing how and when to deliver the truth. Expressing ourselves allows us to know the globality of our truth by putting our obsessive thoughts to the test and by confronting them with reality through the feedback of the person listening to us. Well-tuned sounds—therefore appropriate words—have therapeutic, transformative properties.

Clear, honest and loving communication in each one of our relationships creates more authenticity in the channeled messages. Written or spoken communication is a principle of relating, a principle of coordination. It is a vehicle that consciousness uses to travel and connect with others. Since in the inner world everything is related and organized, our relationship to what is external must correspond to the same principles of union and cooperation. Illnesses would then be a broken shard of communication in the human body similar to problems in relationships and in society. Therefore it is important to choose one's words with precision and care, to purify them and sometimes to contain them. We are responsible for the quality of energy that our communications evoke. How are you managing with communication in the spheres of society, friendship and intimacy? And in your professional work or in your work as a channel?

Any choice, exercised through our will, any limiting or positive thought, and any feeling based on fear or on courage—any one of these—constitute an expression of our power and they bring the responsibility of taking on their expression completely and with authenticity. Each decision is carried forward to its manifestation through the representation that our mind constructs from it and through the thoughts that flow from the image formed of it. Subsequently, words define it and lead it into expression.

The throat is physically situated between mental energies and heart energies. If the mind and the heart do not communicate clearly with each other, one will rule over the other. It is important therefore to make choices and to stand behind them through the force of the integration of mind and heart.

> *Faith and the faculty of choice are by their very nature*
> *instruments of creation.*
> *In our lives, we are containers through which energy is*
> *transformed into matter.*
> Caroline Myss

Purifying: Etheric Meditation

It is time to let your soul take flight.
Le Tarot de la forêt enchantée (The Enchanted Forest Tarot)

Your soul, the bird who holds dear your secrets, will take flight only if you have been listening and have understood what she has to say. The purification of the body with ether, the element that is paired with the fifth chakra, allows us to perceive subtler aspects of the higher chakras. Purification is to be understood here as detoxification.

Be silent. Breathe deeply taking several deep breaths. Let go completely. Make sure that your jaws are not clenched. The tongue is free. Relax the nape of the neck with a few gentle movements.

Let the air penetrate silently into your lungs. For this to happen, the throat must be completely relaxed and your intention must be placed there fully. Silence is all that is present in you. All distractions die down in this inner void which is dense and etheric at the same time. Nothing remains but a minute vibration, like a very, very light breeze that subtly envelops you without any apparent movement. Listen to this silence. Feel the desire that this silence fosters for the emerging vibration to expand. It manifests and begins to cradle you...

Out of this vibration there slowly emanates a desire, a dream, a project for you to be, to exist. From this arose the expression: *And the Word is made flesh.* The word is dear to your heart. In the first mornings of the world this same fundamental vibration that joins with you today in the deepest regions of your being—after having been a nothing, a contracted, tight void—this vibration has slowly tried to become a sound. From nothingness there has emerged the One—the first sound, the first word. Then, this sound has multiplied. Today, you are inhabited by this multitude. Life is charged with life, time has done time's work. Words begin to take shape. Your words want to name and love the essence of your soul, of your being. Wish for yourself never again to be silent, never again to hide your heart and your dreams of creation.

Breathe in, breathe out, breathe in, breathe out.

Express your gratitude for the existence of the ether which, like a subtle fire, purifies all toxic energy. Give thanks for the ether which sweeps away limits and contains life in its entirety. Give thanks... Give thanks! While fully letting go!

The Sound Aum or Om

The sacred sound OM, that we generally attribute to the East, finds it western equivalent in the word *Amen:* So be it. May it be this way: I am. I accept.

OM is a sacred syllable, symbol of the infinite and of the *All*, of Supreme Reality. So sacred that it has not had an image or an appellation for a very long time. Now we can use it, but we must never abuse it. As has been confirmed by science since Einstein, all things are a certain vibratory state of energy. OM is the primordial pulse of the universe, the form in sound of the *All*.

Every manifest thing has arisen from this first vibration of sound. In the very subtle, there first was nothing. From this nothing, this void, a thought was formed—that is, the desire for something else, the desire to no longer be alone. Then, from this thought a vibration emanated. Finally, the sound expressed itself and therefore manifested in what we perceive as reality. This was creation. On the plane of an individual, the creation of our life follows the same course. The desire for procreation by our parents—whether conscious or unconscious—gave us our birth, our being, our body. The desire for ourselves offers us the opportunity to be born a second time to a better life and to manifest it in reality.

Chanting OM brings an inner light, a light of purification, of clarification. It allows us to move forward on the path of consciousness toward meaning, toward depth. No longer do we go around in circles, in the void. We get organized and we move toward a goal—a goal that is determined and attainable. The mind and the higher consciousness form the goal. The mind is transformed by this, having been purged of limiting beliefs and at the same time irrigated with more positive and more creative thoughts of happiness. The higher consciousness, the Self, expands outward and connects us to the totality of life. Our inner state becomes peaceful, more serene and more broadly open to the world.

Chanting OM gives rise to new perceptions and to deep understanding of oneself and of life. It organizes our consciousness and directs it toward the meaning of our existence, leading us to a certain transformation. By chanting OM the consciousness turns inward.

The sacred sound AUM or OM makes the chakras turn, animating them. In chanting OM, we express all that we are as individuals and as essential elements of the human tribe. We inhabit ourselves completely.

In the human being, the throat is what carries words. In the energy of the mind, ether is what carries sound and the Word, which means that sound becomes the creator of matter. Ether is close to the akasha and to the mind. Akasha is the aura of the ether. We distance ourselves from the physical, material world and we approach the subtle world by traversing a connector, a bridge. This is the throat chakra, the communication chakra.

The laryngeal chakra is linked to thought-forms, to words, to the Word. These repeat endlessly within us and they shape our lives—for better or for worse. The sound of OM has purifying properties and is capable of purifying and detoxifying the body and the thoughts. It can harmonize discordant frequencies—both those within us and those that attack us from outside. The subtler aspects of the upper chakras require a heightened sensitivity which is why we need to inhabit a free body that is open and purified.

For an Effective and Loving Communication

Chanting OM: The ideal exercise for harmonizing the fifth chakra

The exercise suggested here is a ritual that governs the sacrifice of certain paralyzing emotions.

Even if you know these emotions and have worked with them, they can still have a negative effect on your life. All sounds have purifying qualities but the sound OM has more than others.

This ritual lasts about thirty minutes. It consists in expressing to another person, and at the same time as that person, an emotional charge without using words but only the sacred sound OM. Regardless of the charge associated with the emotion, when it is chanted and offered to the other person, it dissolves. At the end of this exercise, allow a new inner space to enter into your life and your heart.

You can practice this exercise alone by doing it while facing a mirror for example—being aware that you are using a sacred symbol.

If within yourself you find reproaches, resentments, sadness, fear or other emotions that are troubling you, you can manage to really leave them behind by sharing them with respect, by expressing them in an organized, *religious* way. These emotions (It's not that they are negative but that, having been repressed and calcified, they can have a negative effect on your life.) have a chance of de-crystallizing and bringing in beneficial effects though the OM exercise.

For emotions and thoughts that still have a use, that haven't finished bearing fruit in you, through this ritual a movement toward further purification takes place. Treat these emotions and thoughts with infinite care. They are inner realities which have not yet revealed all their richness. The idea is not to get rid of them but to provide real support—the sound OM—to the process of healing and spiritual advancement. The vibrations of OM are very high and they support a deep cleansing of the charge that certain emotions contain. I repeat: "We don't get rid of our emotions, we clean up the charge that accompanies them."

Trance work and work on oneself benefit from this movement of purification. The exercise suggested above is a letting go of old scenarios and a renewal of the expression of new ones. Behind the dramatized emotional charge wounds remain which must be named for in depth healing. Chanting the sound OM renews the meaning of certain emotions or wounds. Eventually, this chant allows them to be expressed with love in a way that is dynamic and conscious but not intellectualized.

In the Course of Your Daily Life

Play your voice like an instrument

Play with your voice. Let your voice be modulated by following your deep feeling. Speak more slowly or more animatedly. Explore tonalities and different rhythms. Observe the effect your voice has on others. Observe the effect that the voices of others have on you.

Don't forget to sing every day and even to take singing classes once a week. Having done that, I can assure you that singing opens the throat and builds self-confidence and the ability to communicate effectively.

Murmur words of love to those you love. Whisper, cry out, raise your voice with finesse. Make your laugh heard right to the corners of the block. Don't hesitate to make yourself heard loud and clear but lower your voice as often as you raise it. Be silent as often as you talk.

Speak to yourself out loud when you are alone and listen from the depths of your heart to what it has to say. Express yourself in a way that is effective, loving and authentic with everyone not just with those you love.

Love the child still present in you, the wordless child, and he will no longer interject himself into your daily life.

Chapter 15

Perceiving

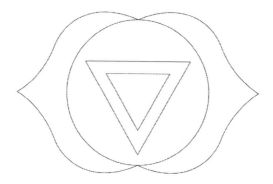

The real voyage of discovery is not in seeing new lands but in having new eyes.
Marcel Proust

Since then, my sight having been restored and my heart renewed, I am learning once again to let Light cradle my life.
Présence, Chapter 2

Being Done with Blindness

False beliefs concerning the opening of the third eye are very widespread: For example, it is widely said that clairvoyance is located in the third eye and its opening is a gift at birth that is impossible to acquire later. It is also believed that only on rare occasions does this gift begin to appear following some serious ordeal or having been struck by lightning (actually or metaphorically!) Furthermore, it's also said that activation of the third eye or *sixth sense* can be an invasive calamity from which it would be impossible to free oneself.

I have said it before and I cannot repeat it often enough: "This faculty is a **birthright**—a skill that can be developed in accordance with one's own wishes." Perceiving subtle energies is a choice. And this choice can be repeated on a daily basis. We can open this kind of intuitive perception at will and close it down at will. There is no need to give an ungoverned clairvoyance the power to run roughshod over our inner peace. We are free!

The third eye is located between the eyebrows and is a secondary chakra of the sixth chakra which is located in the middle of the forehead. The sixth chakra is not limited to clairvoyance but is associated with *higher will* and with the process of introspection guiding us to a more mature self.

A more developed maturity initiates us to wisdom, which allows us to attain a vision of ourselves that is perceptive and aware of a sacred accompaniment. Clairvoyance without maturity is the cause of the bad reputation accorded to the mediumistic arts. It gives rise to many interpretations, projections and power plays. In order that no damage be caused by the perceptions of the third eye and by the communication of those perceptions, the sixth chakra—the accredited orchestral conductor of our inner music—must be harmonized.

Our mind's perceptions must be rooted in our body and in our heart. They must be integrated into the totality of our being and not left stuck at only a mental level.

Living in Your Inner Dwelling Place

Finding answers to our questions brings us temporary peace. Learning to love the questions brings us a peace that is complete.
Marie-Pier Charron

What is my inner space made of? How can I fully inhabit it? How am I going to redecorate it, change it around, transform it, and flourish within it? In what way does it resemble my physical residence?

Am I capable of creating a life that allows me to be at the service of my happiness and to participate in the healing of humanity and of the planet? Am I willing to do what I know needs to be done? Do I have the will and insight I need in order to develop greater wisdom?

Let us imagine for a moment that this inner space is a house, a big, beautiful house that is all our own. In fact, our physical living space is made in the image of our inner world. Discovering resemblances between the two will allow us to assess our progress toward the sixth and seventh chakras.

Physicality: Foundations, rootedness. Where am I at with this? What is the next stage in the harmonization of my first chakra? What is the state of the foundation and of the footings of the house I am living in? Where am I at in my relationship with nature, with Mother Earth, with humanity? Is my lifestyle ecological? How is my emotional ecology? Do I know how to economize my energy for things that I really value? Do I spend energy, time and money uselessly? Do I say yes to myself before saying yes to others?

Relationship Territory: How am I doing with my love life and specifically with each of my relationships? Where am I at with decorating my bedroom and the spaces where I entertain others? How would I describe the intimacy? Do I experience emotional intimacy—whether in friendship and/or in a loving, sexual relationship?

Personal and Professional Development: What improvements are needed in my kitchen, my dining room, and my bathroom? How am I treating my body? How do I nourish it? How and with what do I nourish others? What is my spiritual food? Where am I at with integrating the work that has taken place in me? Do those qualities that I have acquired allow me to develop extensively in the professional world? Are my desk and my computer well organized?

Unconditional Love: Do I love this inner abode of mine? As I live there, do I have compassion for myself? With love for and recognition of all the dark areas as well as the areas of light? Is my living space clean, orderly, agreeable to live in, colorful, and well-lit? Do I like living there? Do my family and friends like it too?

Loving and Effective Communication: How is my communication network in my home and outside of it? With the world? Is my communication with others effective? Up-to-date? Loving? Complete? Honest? Something else? Are the windows in my home clean? How is the entranceway to my physical dwelling? Is it welcoming, hidden, neglected?

Clairvoyance: Is the totality of my physical home and my inner domain recognized in all their light and in all their darkness? Is the lighting of my home and light of my inner temple adequate? Are the many thoughts in my head limiting or joyful? Are my beliefs now in order? What vision do I have for my future? Just as the build up of things from the past portends the future, I bring into question the state of the basement and the attic of my residence.

Quest for Life's Meaning: Am I satisfied with my life? Do I have the impression that I'm accomplishing a particular mission on earth? Do I have the impression of having lived to my full potential? Am I willing to do what I need to do to build my own happiness? Is there a more sacred place where I can meditate in my home and a place where I can truly rest?

Relationship with the Divine: Where am I at with my relationship to the divine? With prayer? With my Guides? What is the state of the roof of my home?

Where am I at with my relationship with the cosmos, with the One? Where am I at with that space where there are no longer any questions, no longer any introspection, no longer any duality, and no longer any ambiguity? That place where there is no longer a house, no longer an inner temple, no longer walls, no longer landscapes, and no longer contemplation? Where there is only awakening to what is...

Are there rooms in me that are shut up, unlit, locked-dungeons? What are the symbols most often used in my home: Nature, art, family, past, future, religious images or others? For example, on the walls of my kitchen are there pictures of appetizing foodstuffs and colorful objects? Are there photos of double objects or couples in my bedroom? Can you recognize me from visiting my home or my office?

In order to deconstruct your home, you need to have built it up and fully lived in it. In order to let go of the search for happiness, you have to have been happy. Marie Pier Charron helps us deepen this thought in her blog of March 14th, 2011. She asks us about what cycles we feel ready to complete. And she adds, "What is the next thing you must do to bring harmony to yourself so you can live the life you desire? What must you do to be deeply cheerful and light? Cheerfulness and lightness are inner states that are cultivated on the inside, but it can be particularly helpful to make changes in our environment."

> *I ask you to be patient with everything in your heart that is still unresolved, and to try to love the questions in themselves, as if they were closed rooms, as if they were books written in a totally foreign language. Above all, for now, don't look for answers that have no way of being given to you— because you would not be capable of experiencing them. You see, everything must be experienced. Experience the questions for now. Perhaps you might come to experience little by little, without realizing it, some far off day, the entry of a response.*
> *Rainer Maria Rilke*

Seeing and Perceiving

The sixth chakra is the master of the body and ensures the transmission of divine energy into the energy system of the human being.

The eyes, connected as they are to the brain, **are the organs of perception of the visible**. Physical reality and sometimes emotional reality, for those who know how to read the body and the face, are perceived through the eyes.

Images are integrated into our mind by a stockpiling of what is seen outside us. For example, we remember certain events or places we have visited or lived in because we saw them. We continue to know and experience feelings of love or non-love for those who have passed or are absent. To do this, we need to look at representations of places, incidents or persons (photographs, paintings and drawings, holy images, and so on). Memories (our image reservoir) underlie our present and construct our future. **Time is transcended.**

It is not only the light that allows us to see and create images. The play of shadows is just as important in storing information on what we are looking at. The form, the structure and the depth of what is around us are visible to us thanks to the shadows. This is how we come to know our physical environment and in part, it becomes our emotional environment. For example, coming back from a walk, we still carry within us the effect of contemplating nature. We may then be happier than before we left and this happiness lasts within time.

The third eye is the subtle organ of perception of the invisible in which inner images form based on our thoughts, our desires, as well as from intuition and imagination. The images prescribe our reality and manifest it, defining our connection to that reality. A thought can be imprinted on subtle substance—the invisible in our deep being—and it can create a visible manifestation. The phenomenon of mediumship is a manifestation of an energetic extension based on intention (thought) that penetrates dense and subtle matter through a subtle organ, the third eye. **Space is transcended.**

The pituitary glands (hypophysis) and the pineal gland (epiphysis) are physical media of support for the third eye. The whole body, in its physical and etheric aspect, is a physical medium of support for the light.

The reflection of the subtle in the physical body is perfect. The pituitary and pineal glands are sensitive to the light, terrestrial light, by means of their denser state and to divine light by means of their subtler aspect. The hypothalamus, thanks in particular to the pituitary gland, plays the role of *orchestra conductor of the physical* in relation to almost all ramifications of the hormonal systems. It ensures the harmony of life systems and allows the nervous and hormonal systems to reach maturity, to attain their inherent wisdom, creating in this way wisdom for the physical being and, by extension, the being as a whole. The body is truly knowledgeable and wise! In its role as an inner teacher, the sixth chakra assembles, recapitulates and projects toward others or gives to others elements of the wisdom it has acquired. It also captures etheric light and subtle forms that collect in it. This material is transmitted to the body. This is one of the reasons why the body becomes the main tool of our mediumistic ability. It does its work in collaboration with our sixth sense, preparing and enlarging space while refining its sensitivity. It supports and consolidates the communication circuits necessary for trance work.

The pineal gland secretes melatonin which promotes sleep and supports access to the unconscious. This gland, which is in the shape of an eye, *looks* upward and captures daily light ever-changing with the seasons. Environmental light is translated into hormonal messages that are conveyed to the body through the autonomic nervous system. The pineal gland also receives subtle and beneficent light during a channeling session. As for the pituitary gland, it *looks* towards the body, bringing order to it and transmitting light to it that has come from above and has been filtered by the pineal! If our consent is lacking however, this transmission can be incomplete causing illness in the physical body or loss of meaning in the mind.

> *...the degree of visual and psychic perception may vary from one individual to the next, ranging from the person who has a heightened sense of observation of the physical dimension to the person who has a psychic gift and can see auras, chakras, details of the astral world, or who can predict the future and engage in distance viewing.*
> Anodea Judith

Getting It Done with Willpower

> *The brow chakra provides the necessary energy for the growth of our inner image, our vision of the world and of ourselves.*
> Ambika Wauters

The sixth chakra, reflecting the action of the pituitary and pineal glands in the body, is the *subtle operations director* of the other chakras. Its opening determines just how one makes the final return to one's inner home territory and it promotes the development of the capacity for self-regulation and self-guidance. Introspection, self-knowledge, self-esteem and detachment are its principal tools. It encompasses much more than clairvoyance.

Taking a look at the world, seeing it and knowing it, looking beyond the visible, beyond the obvious, recognizing the symbolism in each thing, assembling, ordering, directing and managing the elements in our lives, deconstructing the known and limited *me* by abandoning habits and idols that we depend on, leaving our comfort zone—all of those actions—contain the germ of a new birth, a new vision of life, of the world and of ourselves. Then, parts of the *self* are recognized, better known and better loved, are now once again illuminated, reconstructed, taken on and even transcended.

Maturity comes with the discernment and intelligence to apprehend and accept reality in its duality. Maturity means accepting darkness and light and the numerous grays that link them, which are present in all aspects of life. However, without will, all self-knowledge and all work toward maturity can remain barren.

Will is the simple fact of making efforts and keeping going until the final result of what was intended and planned is reached. When will is no longer lacking in our daily life and when its mechanism flows smoothly, *higher will* appears. Thanks to it, we see the connection to the divine in the totality of life and this vision is safeguarded in spite of it being questioned and in spite of the inevitable difficulties we meet on our path of development. Harmony between intention and attention becomes operational. For example, "I undertake as my intention that I will love you since I experience that feeling and therefore

I bring all my attention to bear on how to love you." *Higher will* contributes to the ongoing loving gestures initiated by the intention to love. Intention, whether based on intuition or logic, must be clear. We have to pay attention to what calls us and we need to know how to invest our intention the whole time by agreeing to make repeated efforts. Our life then is no longer something to get done but an enjoyment to be savored!

Opening the sixth chakra or attaining more clarity about ourselves as well as an assertive maturity leads us toward *higher will* and away from control generated by fear and by a vision of being in difficulty with ourselves and with life. Instead of controlling our lives, our *higher will* allows us to participate in life's creation with fluidity.

If we maintain control, thoughts are more involved than is the heart when making a decision or performing an act. Becoming aware of this mechanism can lead us back to the heart and bring out the benefits of thought—if thought is used deliberately. Otherwise, the essence of the life plan becomes cloudy and the individual enters too much into doing and having. We then endeavor to make decisions without being clear about their meaning—without clairvoyance. Hesitation and procrastination set up shop, spiritual guidelines are lost, arrogance is cultivated, separating us from others and from our life mission. Arrogance despises inspiration and rejects accompaniment of the sacred. Arrogance is seeing ourselves as the only instance of a high energy in our lives. It is being certain that we are alone and that we know everything there is to know. This is an attribute of the ego, the limited *self* that we do however need, but which must not be burdensome or tyrannical. It is the totality of certainties on which our actions are based, certainties that sidetrack our actions toward the absence of feelings of love. The *ego* is idolized instead of being mastered and enlightened.

The *higher will*, in contrast, can be a pathway toward the heart. Our project of being incarnated awaits us and we will join with it if we manage to die to our former life and bring our heart energy to our life. There has to be a friendly cooperation with the *higher will* in order for us to do all we can to love living our lives. The ego will not die but will be moved to the side. The last fears will be neutralized as we move into the heart.

In Order to Develop the Sixth Sense

Synchronizing the two hemispheres of the brain is the ideal exercise to support the opening and the harmonization of the sixth chakra

For an Optimal Brain Hemisphere Synchronization:

Standing

1. Turn the head slowly from right to left looking away into the distance without trying to focus on anything.

2. Allow the body to vibrate gently; find the sound of that vibration.

Lying down

1. On your back, rapidly and repeatedly rotate both legs and feet outward and inward. A wave propagates within the body. It cleanses and opens everything along its path.

2. The arms lie along each side of the body and then are raised quickly behind the head. Repeat many times.

The opening of the third eye represents an important milestone in our progress toward our full human potential thanks to a recognized and integrated presence of the divine. One way this opening is brought about, among others, is by the harmonization of the right and left hemispheres of the brain. And obviously, now and at all times, by letting go of the innumerable thoughts that constantly assail us. When the two hemispheres of the brain work together, our vision of reality is much broader. We are still logical but we integrate an intuitive experience into our way of thinking and acting. We become inspired!

The trance state, like art or any work of creation, can be a perfect manifestation of the harmonization of feminine and masculine, of yin and yang, and of the two hemispheres of the brain. A channeled message is the product of this harmonization. The greater the degree of harmony between the polarities within us, the better the message offered to consultants will be. The same will happen in any kind of work, it will be more inspired and life itself will be happier.

Out of habit, we reason: "There's no danger, don't be afraid, go ahead, jump in." Too often our action switch is logic, reasoning. We are identified with our thoughts. To get around that mind, the great sages developed techniques: Breathing exercises, mandalas, asanas, visualizations, mantras, koans. Which of those would you like to adopt? How can you simplify their use by adapting them to our western way of life?

Meditation, prayer, poetry and music represent good health care for the brain just as baths are good for the body. They are simple and effective ways of cleaning up mental pollution and washing away the many worries that live in the head. Besides, we are seeing more and more yoga and meditation courses offered in the workplace. Logic doesn't seem to ever be lost completely. Relaxation and access to the imagination need to enter in to balance it.

Left Brain

Rational and analytical thought, language, realism, compartmentalization. Motor functions. Structure. Discipline. Productivity. Sense of the passage of time. Masculinity. Possibility for planning and manifesting a desirable future. Relationship with religion, with the established order and with the father. Left side of the brain, right side of the body.

Right Brain

Synthetic thought, creativity, intuition, mystical experience, gentle euphoria. Spontaneous and imaginative brain. Experience of the here and now and of a carefree attitude. Sense of the overall picture. Relationship to space. Spirituality. Femininity. Possibility of reconciliation with the past. Relationship to the mother and to Mother Earth. Right side of the brain, left side of the body.

In the Course of Your Daily Life

Seeing with a new eye

Gently tap the third eye, between the eyebrows, about a dozen times before trance work or before taking an important decision. If you feel invaded by too much information from outside your work, place your hand across your forehead and set an intention to close your subtle vision.

When at rest, imagine that your forehead is cool—meaning always ready to see the invisible, to the extent that is beneficial for you. Ask yourself what your spiritual and human values are.

Open all your senses to more refined perceptions. Practice seeing with a new eye. Practice grasping the symbolic message in things and events.

Be confident in others, in life and in the unexpected.

Cultivate detachment. Maintaining therapeutic distance in the framework of all counseling or all teamwork is a very good practice of detachment.

The freedom to come into one's fullness follows the conquest of freedom from having and doing—sometimes all at the same time.

Affirmation for the opening of the third eye: I love myself deeply and I love life—unconditionally.

Chapter 16

Serving

Contact with the light is an act of grace, not something to be consumed.
Daniel Odier

Vibrate, Fearlessly

The seventh chakra is the master of the soul and it ensures the ascent of human energy towards the Light.

A gentle vibration rises from my pelvis, along the whole length of my spinal column. It caresses the back of my heart as it passes upward and sends sparkles through my throat.

As my eyelids tremble and my body quivers, my heart beats more and more quickly but I am not afraid. I have the impression that a breath is animating me without me having to breathe. A light hovers above my head. It will move down into me if I know how to remain attentive. I am alive, that's all.

I am met by an essential energy that is propagated through all things at every moment. Suddenly, it increases. It resonates in me like wedding bells. I am alive and I am certain of it. It's very simple.

I like to settle into this light. It calls me, confirming me as if it was murmuring my name in my ear. It contains me, opens me, holds me, subjugates me and prevents me from fleeing. Joy rises in my open and welcoming body, overflowing with recognition and gratitude for the generous love of this light. I have not even one moment of doubt about its benevolence.

The work of the seventh chakra extends across several dimensions at once, penetrating and emblazoning the infinitely human and the infinitely divine. The final marriage of dualities is a work of art!

"And the light within your Being is expanding thanks
to the love that is well rooted in the earth and desired
by heaven. You are awakening, you are opening your
wings and you are entering into an altered state of
consciousness beyond your physical body. The luminous
wave comes to bathe your etheric body in a golden rain.
You radiate—literally."
Message from Guides

Crowning One Life's Work

For the man who is free, all paths lead to the storeroom
of treasure
Which at first is dark, shadowy, then clear, finally
illuminated
And there, in the center of this empty space, he discovers
the source of life
Alejandro Jodorowsky

Let's imagine, as we have done for a single dwelling, that our
inner world is in the image of a whole village sited at the foot
of a hill. It is dotted with quite a few homes and several little
shops that serve the needs of the inhabitants: The general
store that doubles as a hardware store, the corner restaurant,
the grocery store, offices for the doctor, the dentist, and the
psychologist, the drug store, the post office, the garage, the city
hall and the lawyer's office, the village school, the cemetery
and neighboring farms. No doubt you can also find a church
there or a temple of some denomination or other. The people
of the village are born—they eat, study, work, do business, get
married, make love, have children and raise them, and take
care of themselves. They also pray for good weather or for rain,

for peace and for healing, for happiness and for love. And one day they die. All of this around a church and at the center of the church the storeroom of treasure to be illuminated is associated with the throne room of a castle...

Each house or each edifice corresponds to a part of ourselves. The teacher is represented by the school, the healer by the office of the doctor or psychologist, the nursing mother in us by the restaurant or the grocery store, the organizing and protecting father by the city hall, and so on. The sacred aspect of our lives takes refuge in the church or the temple. That is where we meet the source of life—where the relationship with the divine spreads forth...

Let's take this a little further and imagine that there would be a castle on the hill overlooking the village—its splendor being an instinctive need of the human being, adding scope to our metaphor.

The archetype of the inner kingdom, where a king and queen are enthroned and are in authority, nourishes our psyche and instructs it about a path to be followed, a direction to be given to our lives. This image, repeated in works of art, in myths and fairytales, of the good king—who serves his subjects, resolving conflicts, offering solutions to practical problems and creating peace within the kingdom—inspires us and shows us how to conquer our own monarchy with justice and compassion. Princes and princesses become kings and queens by gaining access to the treasure storeroom, recognizing that their inner work leads them to unification with all of life.

The seventh chakra relates to the sense of beauty, to full presence in the now and the conquest of our inner monarchy or authority. With respect to channeling, the opening of this chakra allows our Guides to make themselves known in a sacred accompaniment. With respect to work on oneself, this chakra crowns the culmination of that work. It is the glory of the human being. Through the activation of this energy wheel our Higher Self connects to the universal.

That doesn't mean that we are not to continue along the path or that we have arrived; it simply means that the path we have been following is leading us to awakening or to a more elevated, wiser version of ourselves. In fact, the opening of the seventh chakra has us make a quantum leap and leads us to a new stage of life that entails even more responsibilities. Like a king or queen who, following coronation, must master their royal power daily to deserve their crown.

A whole lifetime is needed to transform our intimate world. What is there in our heads that remains, useless, waiting for the alchemy of our opaque substance to be completed.

I sometimes have the clear impression of being complete, round and perfect... for the space of a few seconds. It makes me smile, and then someone opens a door, a bell rings somewhere or I start chewing on some obsolete thought and once again I am imperfect.

Golden Light
Only that is capable of resonating
At the heart of our cells
So that the inner leaden substance
Finally is transformed to gold
Installing the verticality of a sacred union
Heaven and flesh now at peace

Marguerite Voltaire, extract from her poem "Golden Light"

Serving

> *The Indian yogi, striving for release, identifies himself*
> *with the Light and never returns. But no one with a will*
> *to the service of others would permit himself such an*
> *escape. The ultimate aim of the quest must be neither*
> *release nor ecstasy for oneself, but the wisdom and the*
> *power to serve others.*
> Joseph Campbell

For the person who meditates or is awakened, of what use would it be to reach the storehouse of treasure and to enjoy its light if there were not also a return to that person's brothers and sisters of the earth? Rarely have I come across the idea of service in writings on the seventh chakra.

Spiritually, the opening of this chakra approaches awakening— that state of total presence to what is. From a simply human point of view, its opening makes our thought more capable of expressing its power.

In channeling, the opening of the seventh chakra refers to the art of transmitting messages, inspired by our Guides, to those consulting us. In training sessions, I often say that we are not doing this work for our own benefit but to serve the person who is asking questions of a higher energy. We are not serving our Guides or ourselves; we are at the service of the person consulting us. Above all, we are not doing this work to gain power over others.

Serving humanity with kindness, compassion and clarity of mind demands that we learn how to serve our personal subjects well. In the inner village that our soul inhabits, each citizen has the duty to become responsible in relation to the others so that the personality becomes integrated and therefore becomes capable of doing humanitarian work and giving its riches to humanity as a whole. *It takes a village to elevate a person to his true nature.*

This is the spirit in which I created a serious training program for individuals who want to put what they have acquired from their relationship with the divine in the service of their clients. I no longer remember where I read this sentence but it is so right that I must share it: "Being divine, we can divine."

In channeling, we must constantly ask ourselves the following questions: How am I going to deploy my life mission as ethically as possible and with as much detachment as possible? Where am I in my progress toward unity?

Crystals

Why speak about crystals at this point? The seventh and first chakras are energetically connected. In the case of the first chakra, the earth is dense and opaque, cold and damp, brown or red and very physical. In the case of the seventh, thanks to work on oneself, the inner earth has become more subtle, more transparent, more colored. It is charged with all the world's memory. It has integrated different aspects of life on earth. Pieces of earth became crystals— precious or semi-precious stones. Their energy is transcendent like ours. The soil transforms into diamonds!

Crystals amplify consciousness. They are one access key to the akashic records. They elevate or help elevate the vibratory rate that is essential to trance work. They open significant energy portals. For thousands of years they have been known to ensure energetic protection. This is what gave rise to the wearing of jewelry. As Judy Hall explains in *Psychic Self-Protection: Using*

Crystals to Change Your Life, crystals are "imbued not only with their own inherent properties but also the power of intent, expectation and long tradition... Color is essentially a vibration of light and the human body is innately sensitive to it." She adds that even though crystals can seem solid, in fact they are an effervescent mass containing much more space than matter.

Consecration of a Crystal

Place crystals in the rooms where you work or meditate and ask that the energy stored in each crystal be transmitted to you, that it be available during your channeling or, as need be, in your daily life.

Purify them, activate them, recharge their energy. Consecration takes place as they are cleaned. Ideally you should have one for each chakra.

Certain crystals have a more masculine energy, others a more feminine energy. Learn to recognize their essence and make use of them judiciously. You need only hold them in your hand to hear their message...

Feel the union with everything which crystals are part of. Feel the earth's love through the crystals that she offers us. Speak to her of your gratitude for the abundance of her gifts.

Cleaning, different methods

- Wash them in salt water, or immerse them in salt water for 24 to 48 hours unless they are water soluble.

- Place them on salt or on brown rice or on a white cloth made of cotton, linen or silk for 24 hours.

- Expose them to sunlight or moonlight (one day and one night).

- Exception: Crystals are delicate, some more so than others. Those with strong colors should not be exposed to sunlight or they might lose their brilliance.

Consecrating

- Hold the crystal in your hands.

- Imagine it enveloped in light.

- Feel its energy; receive that energy.

- Formulate an intention related to trance work or related to a wish or objective that you are pursuing. Speak your formulation out loud.

- Take it to your heart or place it on your heart and thank it.

Always take care to put away the crystals. Left lying around, their energy becomes stagnant or worst, they can absorb negative energies. Be sure to wrap them in little bags of soft material.

> *It is known that crystals store intentions or information that we can place in them. This is well known by scientists who have created watches, computers and the intelligent chip using crystals.*
> Little Grand Mother

For a More Committed Service

Meditating: the ideal exercise for opening the seventh chakra

Meditating means giving up thinking in order to begin contemplating the present. Our thoughts are almost always directed toward the past, holding on to it, reactivating it or toward the future onto which desires and fears are easily projected. We think about such and such a person who hurt us or about some event we really liked, such as our last trip for example—things that have no relation to what's happening now. Or we seek to plan a future that is more reassuring or filled with newly developed relationships that finally are going to be happy ones.

More often than not we despair about the present. Oh, bring on the Fridays, the holidays, retirement! Let that dream take over completely! May our desires be met and may stress be calmed once and for all! May the world finally conform to our illusions!

Recalibrating our useless and paralyzing thoughts is the first movement toward contemplation. Without contemplation of the present freed from thousands of thoughts, both positive as well as limiting thoughts, service to humanity is loaded with sadness and dissatisfaction. It would be best to silence all these constantly repeated thoughts that are chewed over in bitterness, harped on with resentment or with a lack of realism. It's well known—everyone else is wrong: The boss, the parent and the life partner more than anyone. And life too—life never provides enough—why can't it see how neglected we are?

I suggest that you note down some of your malevolent and burdensome thoughts—not all of them, since we have more than

50,000 a day, but identifying them by category: Those connected with the workplace and the well-known incompetence of coworkers, those that criticize family members and others that denigrate even close friends. Those that blame the temperature for our laziness, those that obliterate the day that is today, those that cultivate dreams, fleeing headlong away. And so many others... Committed to paper, their ability to intoxicate us shows itself more clearly. And we begin to have more power over them. The space inside gets bigger because it is emptier and the contemplation of our life in the present begins to bring clarity to our days.

Another list to be made? Yes, that's what I mean. If you don't want to write, remain vigilant and at least take mental note of your thoughts and their wanderings.

In the Course of Your Daily Life

Candles and Crystals

Play with the light in all its forms: Daylight, strong light, subdued light, moonlight, candlelight.

For a certain time, cook with a candle lit nearby. Make love in candlelight, write your diary with a candle at your side and so on.

Provide your trances with a candle—or two or three. Like crystals that you place near you, candlelight is not only a symbol—it is a real protection. You shouldn't do without it.

Meditate with your eyes open in front of a white candle and notice its flame change with the elevation of your vibrations. With time, the flame will begin to speak to you... And you will learn to decipher its language!

Always keep a crystal or a few crystals close at hand, in your pocket, on your work desk, on your meditation altar, in the channeling meeting room, on the counter or near the window in the kitchen as you prepare a meal. Amethyst, alexandrite, diamonds and shattuckite open and harmonize the crown chakra.

Appendices

Thoughts on Ethics

Training in Channeling

What Others Say about My Work

Appendix 1: Thoughts on Ethics

> *From the moment when the therapist is imbued with*
> *a simple and spontaneous love and when it has been*
> *shown he is capable of transmitting it, he is no longer*
> *fighting an illness, he begins to nourish health, and*
> *therefore life.*
> Daniel Meurois

If sessions are being offered in channeling or therapy, whatever the approach may be, certain qualities, certain ways of being and doing must be sought out that indicate the presence in the facilitator of an ethical sense animated by solid moral values.

The channeler must embody professionalism, authenticity and transparency. Channeling is a real therapeutic process that must respond to certain criteria for the light to be distilled through the message that is offered and for the message not to do any harm. By showing a lot of respect for the client and remaining very grounded allows this work to be integrated into the stream of beneficial alternative approaches.

Through energy readings, body work, energy treatment, or the messages provided in channeling, practitioners become therapists in the full sense of the term *care-givers*. They need to keep the expression of their art firmly connected to a knowledge base that is constantly being enriched.

Clairvoyance and its variants as well as channeling offer a sacred accompaniment along the inner path being followed by the client. Is the sacred accompaniment sufficient? Is the collaboration between the channeler and the Light a good one? Talent alone or good technique are not enough. An open heart is not enough either. The therapist or the channeler must show himself to be **capable** of transmitting the simple and true love with which he is imbued.

How **to be**? The practice of the art of healing is more the result of a state than the result of an action. In any therapeutic approach, whether energetic or spiritual, healing takes place due to a resonance between the state of the patient—who seeks *patiently* to communicate his pain and his existential questioning—and the therapist's state of open, loving and authentic presence. In channeling or in spiritual healing, a very important third vibration joins this facilitator/client dyad—that of Beings of Light. Is the trilogy created in this way harmonious?

How **to do**? How to find a way to act and to give messages in channeling so that the opening of the heart finds a rightful and healing expression in this work of collaboration with higher vibrations?

I have identified ten avenues to be pondered, ten basic elements which are to be found in several distinct approaches within somatic, energetic, psychotherapeutic or mediumistic therapies. I am presenting them for you here as an incomplete working document, to be worked on and worked again—with others or by individuals on their own—to be refined, discussed, questioned, and completed. You can make amendments, additions, withdrawals, commentaries and, of course, add your own experiences as patients and therapists, consultants and channelers. My observations are articulated around ten major topics and are not exhaustive. They are set out here as an integrative approach to the basic elements of the therapeutic process.

With each of the proposed ethical concepts, a questioning is outlined on the values that underlie the facilitator's actions.

In offering messages of light or in opening ourselves to the work of clairvoyance, we owe it to ourselves to question our objectives. Our personal power has created our life and will determine the future of our planet. We need to awaken to a new human and spiritual ethic in which the values of the heart come first: Wonder, gratitude, compassion, courage, humility, patience, confidence, etc. Are you familiar with the values in which your trance work is rooted?

If you are someone looking for therapeutic help, in whatever approach that may be, ask about the values, knowledge and competencies that support the work of individuals you consult.

I. Heart Presence

Love is not an emotion, it is a state created by a certain vibration and it is essential that we know how to re-create it at will.

The opening of the heart is acquired as we move through life, encountering joys and ordeals, and also thanks to numerous victories over the very busy mind. Knowledge and competencies accumulate through training, reading and work experience. In order to be able to transmit love, all these elements must be present.

We have to be able to put ourselves in a certain *state of mind*. We could even say in a certain *state of soul*. As if we could touch an inner switch and turn a particular light on or off. The light to be turned on is compassion, intimate closeness and a contact that is both full of human warmth and professional at the same time. The light to be turned off is that of personal emotion that disorganizes—an emotion of anxiety or closing. Also an emotion of judgment and labeling. How to display a professional attitude without passing oneself off as an expert in the other person's life. How to avoid exerting power over the other person?

Heart presence is a state that we induce through an inner silence and through slowing down. The sacred space of the heart, which we were well acquainted with in childhood, is to be found again. It is built in tranquility, in calming the mind and within the intention to serve.

2. **Flexible Structure**

Improvisation cannot produce the same results as an intentionally adopted structure. Also, we need to choose the elements that illuminate the meeting and ensure its quality: First of all, energetic cleaning of the location before the meeting takes place (see Chapter 8); then, proceeding to the trance induction and bringing care to the contact with the person arriving for their consultation; finally, offering a summary of the message if that is appropriate.

First contact:

Very important. The first contact ensures the development of a feeling of security for the client and for the channeler. It provides essential information for a satisfactory unfolding of the message. It is at this moment that the exchange of a few words provides pathways for perception and creates a container for the continuation of the trance and the message. Is the person coming to consult you nervous? Emotionally charged? Open? Welcoming? Resistant? Wary? Skeptical? Tired? Alert? For the moment, just take note mentally.

The message itself:

Inspiration and knowledge come from the Light, the format of the message comes from the channeler, and the collaboration between the two creates an inspired and helpful message. The ears are alert and the listening to yourself and to the other person is active. Remain very close to yourself and to the perception of the energy—the atmosphere—that forms within the new relationship being established from the beginning of the meeting on. Remain very close to the other person. As if antennas were open and the extension of the hearts of the ones and the Others creates a security bubble around the trio formed by the client, the channeler and the Light Beings.

Some pointers on the progression of the message: Do not be forceful, don't upset the rhythm, guide it toward something positive, provide a complete explanation of the symbols, relate things to the human level, suggest exercises to be done, something practical, *a creative action conducted in the real*, as Jodorowsky would say. Don't end up wanting to save the client.

Perceive where the client is standing and speak the same language as him. Don't distract the client from his search for meaning or from his emotions. Don't overwhelm the client session with too many words and too many different directions.

Helping integration, if necessary:

If possible, provide a reformulation and summing up at the end of the meeting.

Highlight some things to work on. For example, "My Guides seem to want to lead you in such and such a direction in connection with such and such an issue."

Help the person to take responsibility for himself. Validate the person's needs and experience in relation to the meeting.

At the end of the meeting, don't stray from the essence of the message by talking too much, explaining too much. Don't discuss the message too much.

Be concise so that the client doesn't end up falling into too much thinking.

3. Emotional and Somatic Experience

Your observation of your own emotional and somatic experience as well as that of your client must be simple, direct and in the moment and it must continually be renewed.

No perception is definitive. From one meeting to the next, with the help of life, the person can evolve a great deal and no longer correspond to the first impression you might have had of them. Each meeting is in the image of a precise moment, delimited in time, like a photograph. Each of us is new each morning, in each meeting—the channeler too. Even within a single session there is the possibility of great change. Bring a specific attention to the body. That is where all healing comes about.

4. Direction of the Message

Remain in the concrete, in the present, staying very close to what the person says, even if it's about the past. For the channeler, what is present is the expression of this past. Avoid intervening in all sorts of directions. For example, leading the person toward your own experience is not appropriate most of the time. Sometimes yes, but not often. Another example: Don't propose the tool of forgiveness when a client expresses anger. Wait, and know how to choose the right moment to do that.

Identify your own emotion that perhaps leads you to *flee* or to want to change what is there, wanting to save the person from their problems or from their anxiety. The human direction is often more spiritual than the spiritual direction.

5. **Centering**

The presence to be offered is not only a heart presence. It is also a presence that is authentic and centered in oneself while maintaining a clear, unobstructed vision of the other person. Centering helps to develop a skill in remaining separate, differentiated, from the client. Learn to not react to the reactions in the other person and to take charge of your own emotional responses so that you can intervene in an appropriate way without judgment. A presence that is not anxious when faced with anxiety or suffering in the other person does not lead to indifference or backing away. On the contrary, the engagement can be experienced more vividly when one of the partners in the therapeutic relationship feels no need to interfere in the other's behavior but instead remains centered and open.

6. **Grounding**

Always be aware of your feet, their extension down into Mother Earth and the support you receive from the Earth. Structuring your work well ensures your grounding and your contact with reality: The place where you meet, respect for timing, not revealing the personal. With experience, there will always be time to relax the structure.

If the boundaries are too imprecise, if the emotional state becomes too exuberant, a lack of engagement is produced that creates a certain anxiety, a backing away and an impulse to change the other person or the unfolding of the message in a reassuring manner.

7. **Active Listening**

Listen with authenticity to the other person just as much as to the Guides. Listen with your whole presence.

The message is pure and simple: No interpretation, no advice, no judgment, no arbitrary interference, no promoting yourself as a model. Judgments can slyly insinuate themselves into rationalizations.

Be watchful that you do not invade the other person with a honeyed tone, or with too much expression of compassion, and not with a harsh or authoritarian tone either. Avoid too great a flood of words and words that are not exact. Pare down your words: "May they be impeccable," as one of the Toltec agreements suggests.

Avoid the traps that the other person necessarily must manifest at certain moments. Ward off his/her defense mechanisms such as denial, humor, judgment, rationalization, resistance, attachment to habitual roles, ready-made responses, taking over the meeting, and a certain kind of projection.

8. **The Ego's Part**

Put less of an accent on performance and the spectacular and more on a real encounter. Maintain the intention of leading the client to her own strengths. Detach yourself from the need for the message *to succeed, to get through at any price* in order to prove your competency, in order to reassure your ego.

It's not about trying to convince or explain, and not about validating yourself or your own point of view. The message remains simple and inspired. The ego has its part to play. If it is solidly constructed, it allows you to have enough self-confidence to open properly to the presence of your Guides. Note that the message itself comes by way of the heart, not from ego.

9. **Transference and Counter-Transference**

It would be naïve to believe that there won't be any transference in trance work and that transference happens only in other therapies. Any emotional experience can be *discharged*, so to say, on the person who is in a position of authority: Professor, massage therapist, therapist, boss, teacher, and even the medium or channeler.

Transference is a necessary bringing into play of certain relationships and their issues. In a way, it is a projection onto the other person of one's own inner psychodramas. It is a positive and fertile impulse from the deep being of the person who is seeking to bring into his life feelings of love for himself while using the other person as a conduit. In contrast, a defense mechanism constitutes an obstacle to this love.

Counter-transference is the reactivation of the unconscious in the channeler. If the channeler feels too much sympathy, annoyance or a desire to save the client, she must question herself, come back to herself and get hold of herself with respect to what cannot possibly be something that belongs to the client.

10. **Inner Space**

Be fully aware of the intimate, mediumistic relationship in which personal disclosure has no place but where the heart dares to fully open—and with compassion. Control only the structures of this space, not its content. Do not try to experience it as a personal or social relationship or even as an amorous and sexual one. That would divert the client from her own search for meaning and healing. The professional ethic requires a purity of intention and experience in the trance work.

The therapeutic space in which the client must be immersed is his own inner space. It is intra-mind not inter-relational.

Appendix 2: Training in Channeling

The art of listening to the invisible world and of transmitting its messages requires preparation and study more than talent. It flows from a choice made with clarity.

A channeling, or reading of subtle energy by a medium or channeler, is a meditation that is open to the Love that leads the client to his own intuition, to his creativity and his intimate divinity. Channeling is a ministry of love and the heart is its sanctuary.

When a channeling takes place, I enter into a deep and conscious trance and I work in concert with the Energies of Christ Light that are present under the name of Joshua. A channeling is like a conference call. I remain present at the same time as I make myself available to the *Higher Self* which is a channel for listening to the invisible world and which in fact is attuned to Unity. The Christ Energies inspire me, loaning me their words and their perceptions of the client in the work of accompaniment that is of a spiritual and psychological order.

The messages received are not focused on predictions even though that does happen on occasion. My work is a work of raising consciousness and of healing. I have developed a skill in opening the door to higher and more loving Vibrations and in creating a bridge between the tangible and a beneficial Intangible. In this way, a process of deep healing of the human heart can be accomplished using information of a spiritual and psychological order. My training and professional experience in clinical sexology and in psychotherapy enrich the messages that come through in a specific way as does my education.

It is my wish that my work—with individuals or in group training sessions—be rooted in the present and in a fully human life. In order to become a helpful channel, first and foremost, purify the view you have of yourself and of life so that the seeing of the subtle energy remains healthy—holy I could even say—expanded and vivifying.

The training sessions that I offer are therefore structured in a way that is both psychological and spiritual around a work on oneself, around an evolution toward more and more grounding, and around a certain acquisition of knowledge about human nature. The teaching is oriented around an empirical axis: Hands on reality; heart turned toward the Invisible. Meditation, observation, experimentation, subtle perception and sharing are its principal means of apprenticeship.

Several participants will not practice the art of channeling in the way I do but will feel that their personal and professional lives become more satisfactory. In this sense, my training, like my book, is open to all. Some people sign up to travel into their inner world during the course of a year with a support group in which spirituality illuminates life and healing work takes place.

The first weekend of the training is an introduction to the training as a whole and to better grounding (first chakra). The following six weekends have as their central theme the next six chakras— their opening, their stabilization and the integration of this work into daily life. The main theme of the residential intensive at the end of the training is the eighth chakra, the chakra of spiritual healing. Practice sessions in channeling are part of each weekend.

At present, my training sessions take place from the month of December until the month of October of the following year. The first three-day intensive happens in December. Five weekend sessions follow at the rhythm of one per month from January until May. There is a break during the summer to foster integration of the learning up to that point and so that the participants can conduct their own initial free sessions of channeling. We meet one more time in September. Then the final three-day intensive takes place in October and includes an introduction to ritualized channeled healing as well as completion exercises to bring closure to the training program.

However, in 2017, I will offer the same training in a residential 7-day intensive format. Detailed information is available on my site: www.carolinecoulombe.com.

My goals:

- To help each person being trained to develop the tools necessary for the opening of his mediumistic channel and for the personalization of his messages so that they are structured, inspired and authentic.

- To allow each person to pursue his own path of personal growth, to re-appropriate his own full strength as a human being, and to experience his spirituality with even more happiness.

Appendix 3: What Others Say about My Work

"My heart is full of gratitude for the woman you are and I have great respect for the medium in you.

"I have seen you as an orchestra conductor minus a baton. You know very well how to be a director using the power of your presence and the force of your intention, always with benevolence and in complete humility. It was a pleasure to share your passion and I feel hugely blessed to have done so. You have conveyed a sense of the sacred to me.

"Thank you as well for the numerous keys you left for us in our journey together through all those initiations. You have helped me to reconcile myself with my humanity which gives more room for the divine within me."
Cécile M.

"My meeting with Caroline Coulombe was a milestone event in my life. The journeying that took place with her gave me access to pathways I had longed for and some whose existence I had not even suspected! The awakening and development of spirituality can take many forms. Within the framework of the training that she conducted, it was, for me, under open skies shining with the stars of openings, sharing, and fraternity. In this way, I was able to reach that space which intimidated me while still being strongly present and vital. This expedition, which unfolded sometimes with intensity, sometimes very gently but always with sure steps, represents one of the most beautiful journeys that I have ever had the opportunity to accomplish along my pathways of the Heart. Thank you Caroline.
Jean-René A.

"For almost three years now, based on a session about every three or four months, I call on Caroline's services in order to be guided by the Light Beings that she channels.

"Beyond predicting an always changing future, They are of precious help in understanding my current life. I would say even that They help me accelerate my process of evolution or rather They help me to not waste time by giving me tools, exercises, visualizations, phrases to repeat and other advice. By responding to my questions, They make me aware of certain aspects of my life that would have taken me more time to understand on my own. In this way, They act as catalysts for me.

"For me, these Beings are real therapists, full of love and light, never judgmental and always respectful of my life choices. Following each channeling with Caroline, I feel enriched with a more vibrant energy. By putting their judicious advice into practice, I notice that my life takes the desired direction and my dreams come true, one after the other! Nothing magical in that except for the quality and fineness of what They bring. I continue to maintain the intention of always going toward more light in my life.

"Caroline knows how to accurately communicate the information transmitted to her. Her great ability to listen, her sensitivity, her heart-felt generosity, her availability and all her knowledge mean that, for me, she is a channel of great effectiveness.

"In order to clarify certain nebulous aspects of our lives, to enter into contact with higher energies, for the simple pleasure of giving ourselves the opportunity to penetrate certain mysteries

of our existence, and for many other reasons, entering into channeling is a real gift that we can give ourselves."
Anne Marie L.

"I had the pleasure of dipping back into the journal written during channeling training. The journey was so rich...

"Following the channelings:

"I am here in a totally other space, really somewhere else. I feel like a new-born opening my eyes onto a world to be discovered. The world is there but I don't yet see it with precision. I know that it is sacred, precious. I understand that the light is always pure and that it comes back to me so that I am cleansed and so that I can perceive its different facets with more clarity. I feel like a child who is beginning to write for the first time: The letters are still indecipherable signs, my hand isn't used to holding the pencil and forming letters to become words, sentences, and stories. Eventually, my writing will have beauty. I love this learning.

"I'm aware of the multitude of ways of perceiving and delivering messages. The color that is inherent in each message is found even here. I am fascinated by the relevance and the preciseness of each message as we are sharing.

"I love the journey toward trance. It is a very comfortable place. I had the sensation of being a pillar anchored to the earth and to the sky, and of deploying an enveloping energy while holding a non-intrusive energy—the sensation of being part of a team, of contributing—all of this while still being absolutely within the uniqueness of my inner world.

"My capacity to perceive, to see, to envision the Divine in the other person was reinforced. It seemed to me there is a door opening to a space where I am seeing greater potentialities than those of an earthly life and yet it is with words and being willing to remain entirely on the earthly plane that I am able to express them. Thank you for that.

"Touching the light, even just a part of it, is a privilege.

"Channeling allows me an access, such a privileged access, to Essence. That touches me greatly. How easy it becomes then to love, because Essence is purity and beauty.

"Some inspired prayers for the trances:

"May I recognize the light in each person. May I see my shadow in full confidence along with the feeling of being accompanied.

"Thank you for the presence of my Guides. Thank you for this opportunity that was given to me to grow and to help, to love and to explore. Thank you for the healing which is underway. I am one who sees in the light and I offer that in sharing for the greater good of all.

"At the end of the training:

"A certain space has grown bigger. I feel *seated*, calmer inside, a little more patient. I want to listen inside myself. I want to listen beyond the words spoken, whether my words or those of the others.

"I dove into the training with real zeal and total abandon. I was absolutely confident of being in good hands with Caroline. The impeccability of her words, her professional ethic and her own engagement on the path provided a reassuring framework

in which I was able to experience a most enriching training. Multiple discoveries, whether inching forward or thunderous advances, creative sharing, deep realizations, lightness, humility, transparency. It was a rich and transformative learning, with new light being thrown on the world we call invisible, on my own make-up and on the abilities of each one of the others. A door was opened to a most alive and most anchored spirituality. I am very grateful for having been able to be part of this cohort, in all the light and with gratitude."
Florence C.

"I received several channelings from Caroline over a period of about three years. The contacts with Beings of Light created an opening to myself that I badly needed.

"The first time that I was in contact with Caroline's Guides, I was dazzled by the Light looking down on me. I felt myself to be under a divine spotlight, a looking that was total, so I was finally seen and recognized. Up until that day, I felt such a need for recognition. I felt myself loved and that love helped me to raise myself up. I was even surprised to be beginning gently to love myself.

"Before these sessions, my life no longer had any meaning—at least that's what I believed. I was dead spiritually and suffering greatly on the human level. The first channelings gave me new life. All kinds of therapies had helped me but there was something missing... It was the part played by the soul that was missing.

"First of all, Caroline's Guides suggested becoming aware of my sadness by writing 25 sad stories a page or two long. I took this project very seriously and I cannot say that it was easy. For a week I was nauseous, especially when looking at the horizon. What was taking place in me—I felt it very clearly—was an energetic re-adjustment. I went through fears, doubts. It was difficult to conceive of other planes; other dimensions frightened me, and I wondered if I might be delirious. I began to look for Light Beings everywhere!

"After the first channeling, I cried a lot. There was a long period of moving inward. I had the impression of a deep cleansing of all my cells which, in the end, extended over three years.

"Through specific exercises that They suggested to me, I became engaged in a process of self-therapy which aimed at the resolution of the energetic invasion known in my childhood and the healing of my sadness. Calmly, I managed to contain my hurt, then to let it go. Little by little, I felt more vitality and more lightness. The immense lake of sadness that slept within me is something I succeeded in draining. I was being reborn...

"During one of the first channelings, They spoke to me about my pineal gland, the gland that secretes melatonin and is associated with the third eye. They saw its fatigue and explained the cause of its exhaustion: I cried out constantly to God. These repeated calls were due to a refusal of my incarnation. In my mother's belly, I changed my mind; I no longer wanted to be living here.

"At the beginning of the following channeling, They congratulated me on being more accepting of my incarnation. I began to recognize where I was in all that and that brought me peace. I felt calmer.

"I was experiencing less sadness, I was more grounded, and a work of opening the heart could then be initiated. It was suggested that I accept to *see* the invisible. The Guides said to me, "God himself accepts you.""

"The opening of my heart was accomplished thanks to the acceptance of my femininity and my sexuality. Two things were repeated; they seemed important. First of all, I had to learn to comfort the child in me because her tears were distracting me from my sexuality. Energetically, it was as if the little girl in me was crying so hard that I was unable to relax during a sexual relationship. Also, my heart did not manage to allow itself to be touched by sexual energy. They also said that a karmic memory that was still too active transmitted a danger signal to men. The men respected me enough not to approach me. 'Let your heart breathe, incarnate your soul, love openly.'

"I have become an independent woman who takes greater care of herself and who is more centered. I have also regain my masculine polarity which I had projected outside of me.

"In learning to let go, in allowing myself to be carried by the current of life, by praying, my connection to life has been transformed, and also my dreams by the way. I receive messages at night from my Guides and I am clearly worked upon energetically. In the morning, my vibrations are more elevated. I often see a golden light and I feel numerous presences. I slept a lot and I healed in the same measure. I feel several centuries more mature. I have become a universal being!

"I do not yet feel sufficiently activated in my life mission. But, I am working at understanding and at experiencing that mission. I have gone back to therapy, but this time I have the impression of integrating the luminous messages received in channeling into my therapeutic work.

"In summary, I can say that I am now maintaining my inner life's current and that it is illuminated by Light Beings. On occasion, I affirm myself against them. I say no to such and such a suggestion or exercise. I disobey. It seems to me that doing so refines my will to be human. I know that this is good and in no way inhibits the expression of my faith.

"In my inner world, I have climbed Mount Everest. It was a phenomenal ordeal. I call it the Way of Light. I am becoming more and more who I am thanks to the structure offered during the channelings which acted as a container. I have found my inner sun..."
Manon St-D.

Bibliography

Note: Books in French have French titles followed by a translation of the title in parentheses.

Alexander, Dr. Eben, *Proof of Heaven: A Neurosurgeon's Journey into the Afterlife*, New Deluxe Edition, Simon & Schuster, 2013.

Angelard, Christine, *Les essences-ciel pour le corps et pour l'âme (Celestial essentials for the Body and for the Soul)*, Montréal, Bayard Canada, 2015.

Baudin, Patrick, *La respiration holotropique. Aux sources de la guérison, les états modifiés de conscience (Holotropic Breath Work. At the Wellsprings of Healing, Modified States of Consciousness)*, Paris, Éditions Médicis, 2009.

Bertrand, Pierre, *L'intelligence du corps (The Intelligence of the Body)*, Montréal, Liber, 2004.

Bolte Taylor, Dr. Jill, *My Stroke of Insight: a Brain Scientist's Personal Journey*, New York, N.Y: Plume, 2009.

Since based on her own experience, this is a thoughtful study of the two hemispheres of the brain.

Boucheron, Patrice, *L'Énergie des arbres, le pouvoir énergétique des arbres et leur aide dans notre transformation (The Energy* *of Trees: The Energetic Power of Trees and Their Help in Our Transformation)*, Paris, Le Courrier du Livre, 1999.

Braden, Gregg, *The Spontaneous Healing of Belief: Shattering the Paradigm of False Limits*, London, Hay House, 2008.

Campbell, Joseph, *Transformation of Myths Through Time*, New York, Harper Perennial, 1999.

Chozen Bays, Dr. Jan, *Mindful Eating: A Guide to Rediscovering a Healthy and Joyful Attitude with Food*, Boston, Shambhala, 2009.

Cunningham, Bailey, *Mandala, Journey to the Centre*, New York, DK Publishing, 2002.

Cuomo, Cristina, *La marche, un mouvement vital (Walking, the Vitality of Movement)*, Paris, Éditions du Dauphin, 2008.

De Mello, Anthony, *The Call to Love: Meditations*, Gujarat, India, Gujrat Sahitya Prakash, 1991.

De Souzenelle, Annick:

The Body and Its Symbolism, a Kabbalistic Approach, Wheaton, Illinois, Quest Books: Theosophical Publishing House, 2015.

An extremely rich reference volume to be kept on hand and consulted often.

La Parole au cœur du corps (The Word in the Center Heart of the Body), Paris, Albin Michel, 1993.

L'arc et la flèche (The Bow and the Arrow), Paris, Le Relié Impr., 2001.

Specifically about sexuality.

Pour une mutation intérieure (For an Inner Transformation), Paris, Le Relié Impr., 2006.

De Witt, François, *La preuve par l'âme, un polytechnicien démontre notre immortalité (Proof Through the Soul: An Engineer Proves Our Immortality)*, Paris, Guy Trédaniel Éditeur, 2015.

Dyer, Wayne:

The Power of Intention: Learning to Co-Create Your World Your Way, Carlsbad, California, Hay House, Inc., 2012.

You'll See It When You Believe It, New York, Harper Collins, 2009.

Être à deux ou les traversées du couple *(Being Two, or The Travails of the Couple)*, par Annick de Souzenelle [et al.], Paris, Albin Michel, 2000.

Grof, Stanislav:

The Cosmic Game: Explorations of the Frontiers of Human Consciousness, Albany, NY, State University of New York Press, 1998.

Psychology of the Future: Lessons from Modern Consciousness Research, Albany, NY, State University of New York Press, 2000.

Hall, Judy:

Psychic Self-Protection: Using Crystals to Change Your Life, Carlsbad, California, Hay House, 2009.

Encyclopedia of Crystals, Gloucester, Mass., Fair Winds Press, 2006.

Hay, Louise L. and Kessler, David, *You Can Heal Your Heart*, Carlsbad, California, Hay House, Inc., 2014.

Heartsong, Claire:

Anna, Grandmother of Jesus, Los Gatos, California, Smashwords Edition, 2011.

Anna, the Voice of the Magdalenes: A Sequel to Anna, Grandmother of Jesus, Santa Clara, Calif., S.E.E. Pub., 2010.

Houston, Jean, *The Search for the Beloved: Journeys in Sacred Psychology*, Los Angeles, J.P. Tarcher; New York, Distributed by St. Martin's Press, 1987.

This book is still relevant today and includes several exercises to be done individually or in a group.

Judith, Anodea, *Wheels of Life: a User's Guide to the Chakra System*, St. Paul, Minn., Llewellyn Publications, 1987.

This book is really worth reading. It contains a perfect synthesis of the chakra system and our western way of life.

Jodorowsky, Alejandro:

Le théâtre de la guérison (The Theater of Healing) (Interview with Gilles Farcet—in French), Paris, Albin Michel, 1995, 2001.

The Dance of Reality: A Psychomagical Autobiography, Rochester, Vermont, Park Street Press, 2014.

The Way of Tarot: The Spiritual Teacher in the Cards, with Marianne Costa, Rochester, Vt., Inner Traditions, 2009

Psychomagic, Rochester, Vermont, Inner Traditions, 2010.

Specifically about intuitive work.

The Spiritual Journey of Alejandro Jodorowsky, Rochester, Vermont, Park Street Press, 2005.

Jodorowsky's memoirs of his experiences with Master Takata and the group of wise woman magicians who influenced his spiritual growth.

Jung, C.G., *Memories, Dreams and Reflections*, New York, Pantheon Books, 1963.

Vallée, Martine, edited by,*Great Human Potential - Walking in One's Own Light*, Outremont, Quebec, Ariane Editions, 2013.

Kharitidi, Olga, *Entering the Circle: The Secrets of Ancient Siberian Wisdom Discovered by a Russian Psychiatrist*, New York, Harper, 1996.

King, Deborah, *Devenez chamane (Become a Female Shaman)*, Varennes, AdA, 2011.

Klein, Jean, *Transmission of the Flame*, St Peter Port (Guernsey), Third Millennium Publishing, 1990.

Labonté, Marie Lise and **Bornemisza, Nicolas**, *Guérir grâce à nos images intérieures (Healing using Our Inner Imagery)*, Montréal, Les Éditions de l'Homme, 2006.

Laszlo, Ervin, *Science and the Akashic Field: An Integral Theory of Everything*, 2nd ed., Rochester, Vt., Inner Traditions, 2007.

Lee, Ilchi, *Brain Wave Vibration: Getting Back into the Rhythm of a Happy, Healthy Life*, Sedona, Ariz., Best Life Media, 2008

Leleu, Dr. Gérard, *Sexualité, la voie sacrée (Sexuality: The Sacred Path)*, Paris, Albin Michel, 2004.

Mc Taggart, Lynne:

The Bond: Connecting Through the Space Between Us, New York, Free Press, 2011.

The Intention Experiment: Using Your Thoughts to Change Your Life and the World, New York, Free Press, 2007.

Melchizedek, Drunvalo:

The Ancient Secret of the Flower of Life, volumes 1 & 2, Flagstaff, AZ, Light Technology Pub., 1998, 2000.

Living in the Heart, Flagstaff, Ariz., Light Technology Pub., 2003.

The Serpent of Light: Beyond 2012, New York, Red Wheel Weiser, 2008.

Millman, Dan:

The Life You Were Born to Live: A Guide to Finding Your Life Purpose, Tiburon, CA, H.J. Kramer, 1993.

Everyday Enlightenment: The Twelve Gateways to Personal Growth, New York, Warner Books, 1998.

Miller, Alice, *Reclaiming Your Life*, New York, Dutton, 1995.

Moorjani, Anita, *Dying to Be Me, My Journey from Cancer to Near Death, to True Healing.* Carlsbad, Calif., Hay House, 2012.

Myss, Caroline:

Anatomy of the Spirit: The Seven Stages of Power and Healing, New York, Harmony Books, 1996.

Defy Gravity: Healing Beyond the Bounds of Reason, Carlsbad, Calif., Hay House, Inc., 2009.

Nhất Hạnh Thích, *The Art of Communicating,* New York, NY, Harper Collins Publishers, 2013.

Odier, Daniel:

Tantric Quest: An Encounter with Absolute Love, Rochester, Vt., Inner Traditions, 1997.

Desire, the Tantric Path to Awakening, Rochester, Vt., Inner Traditions, 2001.

Yoga Spandakarika: The Sacred Texts at the Origin of Tantra, Rochester, Vt., Inner Traditions, 2005.

Translation and commentary of one of the most important texts of the Kashmirian Shivaism tradition of Tantra.

Paris, Ginette, *Wisdom of the Psyche: Depth Psychology after Neuroscience,* London, Routledge, 2007.

Peirce, Penney, *Frequency: The Power of Personal Vibration,* [Old Saybrook, CT], Tantor Media, Inc., 2012.

Shoshanna, Brenda, *Zen and the Art of Falling in Love*, New York, Simon & Schuster, 2003.

Teresa of Avila, Saint, *The Life of Saint Teresa of Avila by Herself*, New York, Penguin, 1957.

Tolle, Eckhart, *Practicing the Power of Now, Essential Teachings, Meditations and Exercises from the Power of Now*, Novato, CA, New World Library, 2001.

Van Eersel, Patrice, *La Source noire (The Black Spring)*, Paris, Grasset, 1986.

Wauters, Ambika, *The Book of Chakras*, Hauppauge, N.Y., Barron's, 2002.

Wise, Anna, *Awakening The Mind, a Guide to Mastering the Power of Your Brain Waves*, New York, Penguin Putnam, 2002.

Woodman, Marion, *Addiction to Perfection*, Toronto, Canada, Inner City Books, 1982.

Glossary

Anima

Jungian term designating the feminine part of men.

Animus

Jungian term designating the masculine part of women.

Archetype

Ideal and universally recognized model.

Automatic Writing

Associated with intuition and the first stage of opening all the chakras. Sometimes there is an accompaniment of Light Beings.

Card Reading

(Tarot and others) Associated with symbolic intuition and with the first stage of the opening of all the chakras. Eventually there is no longer any need for a material support such as cards.

Channeling

Collaborative work with Guides of Light. Flows from the seventh chakra. The person channeling—the channel or channeler—is the catalyzer, transmitter, or translator of a subtle energy that is of very high frequency.

Chakra

From the Sanskrit (çakra) meaning wheel or circle. A chakra is a whirling wheel that assembles the life energy of an individual into a meeting point of several energies of various frequencies.

Clairaudience

Listening to subtle energies in which the ears are involved. Associated with better listening on the human plane.

Extrasensory perception carried by the fifth chakra.

Clairsentience

Related to empathy. Extrasensory perception carried by the second chakra. Develops a greater sensitivity toward others and their emotional state. In certain cases, associated with a kinesthetic ability to perceive, meaning that the perception of subtle energy originates in the body.

Clairvoyance

Very refined perception of subtle energy associated with the sixth chakra.

Ether

Includes all the other elements: Earth. water, fire, air. Contains life and makes it sacred. Carrier for sound and basis for the propagation of light.

Hypnogogic

Deep relaxation that precedes sleep and generates greater receptivity in all learning.

Individuation

Jungian term that refers to taking charge of oneself in the development of the Self. The result of this is the integration and acceptance of all parts of oneself.

Inspired Speaking

Associated with intuition. A form of guidance that happens spontaneously.

Intuition

Immediate direct perception of others and of reality in the light of archetypes. Association between the third and sixth chakras.

Mediumship

Opening to parallel worlds. Contact with deceased souls. Flows from the sixth chakra.

Numinous

Energy emanating from a divine presence and opening the way toward mystery, whatever it might be.

Prana

Subtle energy associated with the air. Oxygen's aura.

Psychokinesis

(Synonym of telekinesis) Ability to transform or move objects using thought.

Subtle Energy

Energy whose vibratory frequency is very high. Undetectable.

Telekinesis

(Synonym of psychokinesis) Ability to transform or move objects using thought.

Telepathy

Direct perception of information without going through one of the five senses.

Printed in the United States
By Bookmasters